# DRUG OF CHOICE

The Inspiring True Story Of The One-Armed Criminal
Who Mastered Love And Made Millions

# A SPECIAL THANKS TO:

*My mother, Maria Wijnakker*
*My sisters, Miranda and Andrea*
*My darling wife, Stefania*

*Jim Stark, Ryan Bukevicz, Roan Mooij, Jesse Krieger, Charles Ngo,
Samir Sehgal, Tobi Atkins, Site Steendam, Bas Smit, Kasper van
der Meulen and Hardy Hekelaar*

*Best,*
*Mark*

## Advidi

*Dedicated to Advidi, my preferred affiliate network.
The support and dedication they have provided me has been
priceless - they looked beyond just profits and I'm thankful for
the relationship we've developed over the years.*

# TABLE OF CONTENTS

# THE LAST THING I'LL DO

*I believe, when I'll be on my deathbed, the last thing
I'll do is hit refresh.*

# HEIST

Alvin and I crept through the industrial complex, towards the big building with it's lights still on. It was a sorting facility for the postal service, and we saw a group of kids—only a few years older than us— who were working the night shift toss out their cigarettes and return to work. It was a low paying job for inexperienced, uneducated people. The night had a mist we could feel, shimmering around traffic lights, diffusing reds and greens before reflecting them off of puddles on the road.

Alvin looked tired. His long black hair was wet, and his brown skin was shiny in the rain. We both wore sneakers with holes in them, not that we cared. Baggy pants, t-shirts, and worn- out shoes were a uniform that set us apart from the others. And we were different from them. We always had been. Although we weren't from the same family, or even the same race, we were brothers.

When we reached the building, we strode through the automatic sliding doors and walked right past the security guards. One of them nodded at us, and we nodded back. Kids like us came in and out of the building nonstop. *I'm just a guy going to work. I belong here*, I convinced myself. If your frame of mind is strong, everyone will play along.

The bottom floors were for low-level employees. We stepped into an elevator, pressed the button, and rode in silence to the top floor. There were still a few people working in offices there, but not that many because it was already past midnight. We passed an open office door. An Asian man wearing glasses and a grey suit looked up from his desk, surprised, but then looked down at his computer screen and continued working. Close call.

There was a little fridge in one of the offices with all kinds of soft drinks. We each took a can of Coke out of it and drank them while we looked around. At the end of the empty hallway was the office of the managing director. We went in. I sat in his tall, black leather chair and started searching through the drawers of his desk. Alvin opened a blue metal cabinet at the back of the office.

'Wow, nice!' I heard behind me. Alvin had found a money box, a big one. The small lock seemed like it could be broken without too much force. He lifted up the box and shook it. We heard something moving inside.

We looked at each other, excited, and started searching for something to break the lock with. In one of the drawers I found a huge pair of steel scissors. They looked strong enough. We stuck the scissors through the lock hanger and started turning using our entire weight and strength. It snapped off.

There were stacks of money inside — hundreds, fifties, and tens. We took off our shoes, and put the notes in them under our feet. We were about to leave when the office door opened. A man stood there in the hallway. He was muscular, with a thick brown mustache, and he carried a walkie-talkie on his belt. He stared at us, angry. It was a security guard from downstairs.

He grabbed us both. We didn't put up much of a struggle. We'd have to get three floors down and run past security, so we knew we had no chance. He squeezed our upper arms firmly and dragged us through the hallway. Our arms bruised. We couldn't help but let out sounds that made it obvious it hurt. At the bottom floor he pulled us to the security office where his colleagues were waiting. The sliding front doors of the building were open, and someone was walking out, just a few steps away from us.

Alvin grabbed a stapler that was on the desk, and smacked the guard in the face. Blood gushed out. He grabbed his face and let us go. We both ran outside. He ran after us, but we ran harder. I ran so hard and for so long that my entire body stung. I was scared of jail, but more scared of getting my ass kicked by an angry muscle-bound security guard. When we ran off the terrain we needed to cross a four-lane street.

A woman driving an old red Mercedes saw us running away from security. She hit the brakes of her car and came to a standstill in front of me, deliberately blocking my way. I jumped on the hood of the car, rolled over it, fell off the other side, and kept running, leaving her startled. When I looked back, this guard was still following us.

I got to a tunnel. I knew a hill was on the other side of it, and below that hill was my mom's house. If I could make it to the hill, I'd be home. While running in the tunnel I heard something fall behind me. I looked back and saw the guard had thrown off his walkie-talkie and his jacket so he would have a chance to keep up. Blood still dripped from his face.

The end of the tunnel was in sight. I ran up the hill. On top of the hill I collapsed. I couldn't run any more. I was exhausted. I let myself fall and rolled down the slope. When I came to a stop, I realized where I was — in front of my mom's house. I was no longer being chased. The guard probably kept following the road and didn't see me run up the hill, to the right just after the tunnel's exit.

I was covered in mud, grass, and blood from rolling down the hill. My clothes were wet and stained from the rain. One of my shoes was soaked after stepping ankle deep in a puddle. But I had gotten away.

After going inside, I turned off the lights. I was scared. Alvin had run in a different direction somewhere. I hadn't really been paying attention. Maybe Alvin got caught and he was at the police station. We were already quite notorious in the town of Zwolle, and the police knew we were a package deal. If he was arrested, I couldn't be

4

far away. They might be on their way right now, because they knew where I lived. Someone knocked on the window with three loud bangs. Adrenaline shot through my body. I was sure it was the cops and I'd get arrested now. I looked over at the window, carefully.

I saw a dark shape, a figure with long curly hair. It was Alvin!

He came inside and sat next to me on my mom's sofa. We took the stacks of money out of our shoes and placed them in piles on the glass Ikea coffee table. This was the first time I experienced the feeling of thinking, *I'm rich*. This was more money than I had ever seen!

After this, we had cash to buy brand name clothes, a PlayStation, mobile phones, and throw money around at parties. We were being noticed by fellow criminals in town, and they realized we were no joke. Even if they still did not fully respect us, they figured we at least knew what we were doing.

We had made real money with a real heist.

# THIS IS ME

Some of what I'm about to tell you is far from flattering. In fact, I've hesitated to publish. I'm ashamed of much of it. The way I've behaved and the choices I've made are embarrassing at times, and I'm not sure I even want people to know. But, this is me. Take it or leave it.

I'm typing this while sipping champagne in business class, on my way to Barcelona for a luxurious weekend. My beautiful fiancé is visiting her parents in the mountains, and she suggested I take a weekend off myself. I've been working so hard.

Now, my life consists of taking care of good people, positive people. I'm involved in several businesses. I have employees. I travel the world. I deliver value to people's lives. I give large sums of money to charity.

Violence, crime, and drugs are so far from my current life it's hard for people to even imagine me living under those conditions, and doing those things. But I do remember it. I can't forget.

I hope you'll understand that my beginning was very rough. Luckily I learned to develop myself as I grew older, which cannot be said for many of the people who came from the same place I did. Also this is not meant to make you think I have all the answers. What I hope it makes clear is that not having all the answers is fine. It's actually great to come to terms with the fact that no one has all the answers, and you don't need them either.

By staying curious and constantly learning, you might come to insights others won't. You're not stuck in your situation, whatever it might be. The world is big. There are so many people in the world that possibilities to connect with either positive or negative people are endless. You can choose your environment. You can choose who you want around you. It all depends on your own behavior. Your behavior is a choice.

People in my current life have no idea where I came from, and don't have a clue about the way I used to behave in my teenage years and early twenties. They also haven't known the things I had to overcome to get where I am now. Some people I've left behind from my old life don't understand the person they think I am is gone. He might as well be dead.

Not only did I leave that life behind me, it's now a distant memory. Since then, I have left two other lives behind me in a similar drastic way. Constant evolution is inevitable if you want to move forward. We all learn from our mistakes. So you better fuck up as much as you can as fast as you can, that way you'll learn more and faster than anyone else.

Sometimes when I see people from my old life, they still think I'm the same person, only richer. As if somehow I haven't had to change my own behavior — as if I magically live a completely different life now. That's ridiculous. It's been very hard work. They only see the result, not the progress and the struggle. There are even people existing, still to this day, who somehow hold resentment toward me for the way I was behaving when I just dropped out of high school, or was just released from prison.

What they don't understand is that guy is dead, and I'm the one who killed him. The person I am now came in his place. I hated who I was, and now I even hate people who are like the person I used to be.

Today, I don't really live anywhere. I travel nonstop, more by plane than by car. I spend most of my time in Hong Kong, Spain, the UK, and the United States. My friends include business moguls, life coaches, bankers, professional actors, and athletes. I've helped thousands of people better their lives during the journey of improving my own.

But that's today.

We're talking about then.

Before I moved to Zwolle, I was innocent.

In Zwolle, I became fucking feral.

# A BAD MOVE

I was born in The Hague, Netherlands, in August, 1982. It's a big city near the North Sea. My childhood memories are of large streets filled with traffic, parties, and summer days spent playing on the beach with my two sisters and mother, building sandcastles and catching crabs between the rocks beneath the pier.

When I was five years old, I woke up in a hospital bed, and saw my mom sleeping on one of the chairs. 'Hey Mommy' I said. My mom opened her eyes. 'Oh Mark, you're awake!' she screamed and hugged me. 'HE'S AWAAAAAKE!' she shouted towards the open door. Her voice echoed through the hallway. A doctor and two nurses came running in and told me to lay back in my bed. They started measuring my blood pressure and pressed a cold stethoscope against my chest and listened to my heart. 'He seems to be fine' the doctor said while shining a light in both my eyes.

'Mark..' the doctor sat down on one of the chairs and looked me in my eyes, 'do you know what has happened? Do you remember?' 'No,' I answered. 'You've been in an accident' he continued. 'You were hit by a train and it ran over your arm. Look, your arm is gone.' He pointed at my right shoulder that was wrapped up in bandages. My entire right arm was missing.

'Will it grow back?' I asked him with a smile. He shook his head. I looked at my mom, she was in tears. She shook her head. 'Ok..' I said, 'can I go home now? I'm hungry. What's for dinner?' My mom smiled. 'You'll have to stay here for a few weeks' the doctor said. 'The nurse will bring your food in soon.' 'I like white bread with peanut butter please.' 'Of course,' the doctor answered.

I hated the hospital. After two weeks, the doctor let me go home because I was causing trouble. It did not take me long to get used to this situation. As a kid I accepted it and moved on with my life like nothing had happened. I never really saw this as a big deal. I grew up doing everything all the other kids were doing, never even realizing there was anything different about me. When I was seven, my father got a job in Zwolle, a little town in the east of the country, and we left The Hague behind. It was exciting to me. A completely different city.

I call Zwolle an insignificant little village now, but the people born in Zwolle get offended when I do. To them, Zwolle is the capital of the province, and thus a big city. They don't realize the whole province is littered with little villages, and Zwolle just happens to be the biggest one.

Zwolle was made up of canals and old churches and a very small city center with a few shops. There was a big church tower in the middle. This was the pride of the city, they even had a song about it. It had a round roof, a clock I'm not even sure worked, and a lookout balcony from which people liked to jump to their deaths. Today, there is an 'anti suicide safety fence' around it. It had a crucifix on the roof, with a gold colored rooster on top.

On Sunday, all shops were closed in Zwolle. They wouldn't open again until Monday afternoon. There was one exception, the 'Shopping Sunday.' The first Sunday of the month a few shops in the city would be open for a few hours. The entire town then came out and crowded the streets of the tiny center. Shopping Sunday was a big deal in Zwolle.

Kids there had a small town mentality, and I was confronted with that right away on my first day of school. 'Why do you talk like that?' They said. 'You probably think you are better than us, huh? With that big city way of talking!' a fat kid mumbled in a farmer's accent.

I couldn't even comprehend what was happening. I had no idea I had a big city accent. I just talked the way everyone I knew talked.

'You think you deserve special treatment because you have one arm?' a slim kid with a booger dripping from his nose asked me while he frowned his eyebrows, trying to intimidate me.

'Uhh... what? Oh... I have one arm? Yeah, now that you mention it, that's true... what about it?' was my reaction. I had no idea why they were behaving the way they were.

The fattest off the group started pushing me. I took a step back each time he did. 'Come on, fight me, pussy. What? Are you scared?' I had never been in a fight. I didn't even know why the hell I would. I mean what would that solve or prove? It was all very confusing to me, but one thing was crystal clear. I didn't belong there.

I was a soft-hearted kid. I was never confronted with aggression, never had to physically defend myself, had never been picked on, and never picked on anyone else. The way these kids settled things was apparently by fighting it out. I got the feeling these kids were plain retarded. The whole town looked like they were in on it though. Soon, I had the outspoken opinion that the whole town was retarded.

These people were just dumb, in my opinion, just dumb. I hated these dumb people. *It's ok that you're not smart, but don't pretend like you know everything, you stupid idiots!*

The first few months in Zwolle I was sad, and I cried in my room a lot. I did not want to go to school anymore and wanted to move back to The Hague where people were friendly. I really felt unsafe in school. I felt that I was being forced to spend time in a room with extremely aggressive kids, who were stronger than me and wanted to hurt me without there being enough supervision to keep me safe. I blamed my parents and the teachers for this.

*How can they do this to me? What did I do wrong? Why am I be-
ing punished?* This went through my mind all day. It pissed me off.
I grew angry at everyone. The other kids in school, the teachers,
my parents, everyone. When my mom told me it was the law in
the Netherlands that children have to go to school, I blamed the
government. School, to me, was not a place to learn. School was a
place of aggression and violence. When I learned how a democracy
works, and that these laws were there because the country voted for
these laws, I started to hate the entire population for sending me to
that terrible place.

# ORIGIN OF VIOLENCE

These kids were violent, and they wanted to test me out. Where my missing arm once was, they saw a weakness they could exploit.

After being picked on and avoiding confrontation for a very long time, I knew something had to be done. I needed to fight one of these kids. But chances were I'd lose. I had never fought anyone in my entire life, and I had only one arm.

One Wednesday afternoon, during the lunch break, one of the bullies started picking on me. All the kids were standing around, provoking, laughing, and I knew no one was going to help me. The teachers sure weren't. They were just standing around, so I needed to help myself. What I also knew, is that I did not stand a chance in a fist fight. My only chance was to grab a weapon and end the fight as soon as possible. I was scared I would get hurt.

The fat bully named Timmy had his back turned toward me. He had his right arm pulled inside in his sweater, pretending he had one arm. 'Haha look at me, I'm Mark!' All the other kids were laughing. I grabbed a brick and called his name. 'Hey, Tim!' He quickly turned around, 'What?!' I smacked him in the face with the brick. *SMACK!* The sound echoed through the entire schoolyard. A thick splatter of blood shot out of Timmy's nose and over his lips. He squeezed his eyes shut and stumbled backward. He tripped over his own feet and hit the pavement with his head, hard.

He stayed down.

I started crying and couldn't believe what I had done. A teacher grabbed me, pulling me inside. He and the principal shouted at me.

'ARE YOU CRAZY!?' A chunk of white, dried-up saliva twitched up and down in the corner of his mouth. I held my hand in front of my face because I was scared it would land on me as he shouted.

'You might do these things in the big city! But over here we are civilized!' he spat.

I couldn't believe it. *Where did that come from?* In The Hague I never had situations like this. In 'the big city' people were friendly. I didn't even want to be there. I didn't want to fight. They forced me to confront them. *They had twice the fists I had. What the hell did they expect was gonna happen?*

It became a habit after this for me to hurt my classmates each time they drove me into a corner. Some kid teased me in the cafeteria. I hit him with a tray. They quietly snickered in class when the teacher turned his back. I flung myself at them, flipping over their table. After a few months of this, they kicked me out of school. The whole town soon knew who I was. Some of the other kids were forbidden by their parents to be friends with me. To them I was an out-of-control city boy who was violent and aggressive.

However, I felt like a victim who was forced into a situation and was doing whatever I needed to survive. The town blaming me for this only fed my anger. No matter what I did or where I went, everyone in Zwolle looked at me funny because of my missing arm, and everyone judged me for it.

If I couldn't do something, people said 'of course' I couldn't do it, and I shouldn't even try because I had one arm. If I could do something very well, those same people would say it was easier to do with one arm.

I lashed out more, and became more aggressive and violent. I kept to myself most of the time. I was in and out of schools, not really paying much attention to what was going on in class, if I even showed up. I would spend most of my time drawing cartoon characters. I loved drawing. My dad showed me how to draw a horse when I was very little, and I had a talent for it. My goal, my number-one focus in life, was to become an artist.

If the teacher was speaking in class, I was drawing. At recess, I was drawing. Drawing and reading comic books was how I spent my time. I had learned that keeping to myself was the best way to go about life in this town. As long as I focused on what I was doing, I would not get into any trouble with anyone.

At such a young age I had learned that violence was the quickest way of solving problems. It seemed like the easiest, and the fastest way to keep people at a distance. It's something I had picked up. It worked, so I kept doing it. Especially when someone mentioned my arm, I would snap. Just the question, 'Hey, what happened to your arm?' would be enough. This could mean just a punch with my fist to the nose, or as bad as hitting someone over the head with a chair.

Getting expelled from school was no longer a big deal. I didn't see any negative consequences in that — just more free time I could spend on my drawings and less bullshit to deal with.

It was behavior born out of fear. This attitude was working. They left me alone, so that's what I kept doing — a vicious cycle.

# FAMILY LIFE

I was twelve years old. My mother was crying in my parent's room. I crept upstairs, avoiding the spots on the stairwell I knew creaked, and opened her bedroom door. She was lying on her bed, holding a piece of paper. She was in tears.

'What's wrong mommy?' I asked.

She quickly wiped her cheeks dry with both hands and said, 'nothing. Come on, let's go downstairs.'

I had the feeling something big had happened, but she wasn't telling me.

That evening, my dad wasn't home. We were sitting around the table, my mom, my two sisters, and me.

'I have to tell you something,' she said. 'Your father has left. He has decided he wants to live with another woman. He left me a note, and he is gone.'

My sisters and I started crying. My mom hugged all three of us while tears rolled down our cheeks. Then she told me who he left her for. I couldn't believe it. It was the stepmom of one of the kids from of my class.

This woman had the reputation of sleeping around, and rumor had it that she broke up several marriages already, including the one of the parents of this kid I knew. It gave me the feeling my dad got played for a fool, and he left us. Not just my mom, but my sisters and me as well. *For this slut?*

She had daughters of her own. Two girls going the same route in life as their mother. So now my dad will be their father, instead of mine? I was ashamed. My world collapsed.

My mom was left to raise me and my two sisters on a nurse's salary. He paid no alimony. I didn't see or hear from my dad for a week. Kids in school started teasing and bullying me more, because now my father had decided to leave my mom for the town whore. I was so ashamed, and angry at my father.

The day after my father left I got kicked out of yet another school for violent behavior. I threw a chair at a teacher, and beat up a kid for laughing at me.

I refused all contact with my father, but he never put in much effort to get in touch with me anyway. He really didn't give a shit. It made me feel horrible. This, in combination with all the other things going on in my life at that time, made me more and more angry and violent.

My dad was the one in my family I had the best contact with. He was intelligent, he was a great chess player, he was interested in art. He was who I wanted to be. I didn't realize at the time, but throughout my life I would look for the same connection in people that I had with my father. Instead, I only found an emptiness, a void he ripped from my being.

I really missed him.

# ALVIN

When I was sixteen, I smoked weed and snuck out at night to spray graffiti on trains, mainly cartoons. To the law this was a criminal activity. To me, it was a creative outlet as well as a way to get back at society.

I hung out in the skate park until late. I shoplifted, burgled, stole cars. My friends were the outsiders, the skaters, the stoners. But I was the crazy one. No one had behavioral problems like I did. No one was as aggressive. No one hated authority as much as I did.

I stopped feeling connected to anyone around me. No one understood me. No one knew what I went through. Even when I was surrounded by people, I was alone. We spent most of our weekends at my mom's house smoking weed.

My mom was not home during the weekends, so we had the place to ourselves. I'm sure my mom could not really handle me. Once, she tried to punish me and started beating me. In the midst of her rage, I laughed, as if it tickled.

There were three guys I called friends: Bas, Frank, and Kasper.

Bas was very tall with short, curly red hair. He talked so much, his mouth never closed. He was always very certain when he said something. Because he read a lot and watched the Discovery Channel when he was stoned, he thought he knew everything. But after he said it, he'd look at me as if seeking my approval, because he subconsciously needed me to know that he was right.

His main problem was that he was too nice to people. Even when they treated him like shit. There was no aggression in him. I found that to be terrible. Sometimes you need to stick up for yourself. He didn't.

Frank and Kasper were brothers. They were both allergic to sugar. Frank was the quiet type. He was short and husky, but extremely strong, and clever.

Kasper was chubby. The fat in his face swallowed his chin and cheek-bones, making his head look like a round balloon with a face on it. He wore glasses. Like all of us, he dressed in baggy pants that hung halfway down his ass. A big chunk of his boxer shorts stuck out up to his belly button. He moved slowly. This was partly because the weight of his fat and his undeveloped muscles were slowing him down, and partly because he was constantly stoned.

He was the most sensible person of the group. Kasper was the kind of guy you could really talk with, and he would give you the feeling he really understood you. He was not judgmental. For some reason, Kasper was the kind of person I had to be honest with. It was a feeling I got when I was around him. The feeling like pretending was futile. He'd see right through me.

All of us smoked weed all day, every day. We listened to rap music and drew cartoon characters on everything. Most days after school we'd meet up, make some fresh mint tea, smoke weed, and watch Cartoon Network. My times with them were great.

Unfortunately, my life took an even worse turn, and my contact with them diluted. I had a fear and anger inside me that they didn't have. It was a side of me I felt they didn't understand. I always felt very alone in that.

One day, a new kid, Alvin, came to visit. Alvin was fifteen years old at the time, and I had never met him before. He was dark-skinned and a little bit taller than me. His curly black hair reached his shoulders.

He wore baggy pants. He had moved to Zwolle just a few years earlier from a tiny island in the Caribbean called Curaçao.

Curaçao is a former Dutch colony, part of the Dutch Antilles just off the coast of Venezuela. It's where the Netherlands kept plantations and slaves they brought over from Africa, which is why the population there is black and speak Dutch to this day.

After smoking weed and drinking beer, I wanted to go out and spray some graffiti on trains at the train graveyard, a few miles from my mom's place. I had a new piece I was working on all night.

'Yo, any of you guys wanna go out with me and spray this thing on a train?' I asked, while holding up a piece of paper with a bright colored drawing on it. Everyone looked around at each other and Frank replied with 'No... uh... not really..'

'Ah come on guys, what are you? Pussies? Let's go. I don't wanna do this by myself. I'll be bored.'

Frank again opened his mouth and told me 'Nah, Mark. I'm drunk, I'm stoned, I don't wanna get arrested now, that would suck. You go by yourself if that's what you want to do. But leave us out of it.'

'Pfff, bunch of pussies..' I said and started filling my backpack with cans of paint.

'I'll go with you,' Alvin said. I looked at him, surprised. 'Yeah, I'll go...' he repeated. I smiled at him.

'Awesome, what's your name again?'

We went out and I noticed something in him I had not noticed before in anyone. He was not scared of police, or anything really, like me. Alvin didn't give a fuck. 'Yeah, why would I care?' he said, 'Fuck these cops dude, fuck this whole town..'

'No one hates this town more than I do, Alvin, Believe me. These fucking dumbasses have been treating me like shit since I moved here..' I told him while walking over the train tracks, and looking around if there weren't any cops on our trail.

'Hand me one of those spray cans' Alvin said, and he started spraying his tag *JEST* on trains as we walked past them.

I continued 'Somehow these inbred farmers here have some issue with me having one arm. Teachers, students, police, it doesn't matter, they are all equally dumb and prejudiced. I wonder if they have some sort of stupid gene in this province.. I never had things like this in The Hague...'

We stopped in front of a parked train. I took out the drawing I made earlier that evening from my pocket, looked at it, and started sketching the outlines on the train using a grey colored spray can.

'Well.. I moved here with my parents when I was ten years old.' Alvin held my bag with cans and handed me each color when I needed it. 'My dad is Caribbean, but my mom is Dutch. But I fucking hate this stupid town. I wish I never moved here.'

'You and me both!'

'Once, a teacher made me kiss his shoes and called me a nigger in front of the class while all the kids were laughing. Fucking assholes.' Alvin exhumed anger from his eyes. 'I'm not even joking. I'd kill all of them if I had the chance.'

Alvin was just as pissed off at this town as I was. The way he dealt with it was similar to me: violence and aggression. 'I'll fucking kill all these pieces of shit when I'll have the chance.' I felt a connection to him I had not felt before to anyone, and he felt the same.

Until then, I had been alone in my anger. The whole town, even my good friends, Bas, Frank, and Kasper, thought I was crazy and there was something wrong with me. However, I felt there wasn't. The town was crazy, if you asked me. I was merely trying to cope.

Loneliness was how I would describe my overall feeling the entire time I lived in Zwolle. I was alone in my struggle and alone in my anger. No one understood me. But Alvin did. He shared my exact sentiment. He had the exact same reaction. I finally had the feeling I belonged.

Everyone else in town was part of a group. They all had friends, and shared a certain brotherhood. I never had that, and I was longing for it. That's what I found in Alvin — not just the brother I was longing for, but also the confirmation I wasn't crazy.

From that day, we were inseparable. *We were brothers.*

Our whole life began revolving around getting back at society. We became the bullies of the town. I became what I hated, but I felt those assholes deserved it. A lot of it was petty crime, like stealing bikes as a form of public transportation. We needed to go somewhere? We stole a bike. We needed to go back? We stole another bike. No big deal really.

We once went to a golf course. We stole money out of their club house and their golf carts. We crashed two of them at the course while we were joyriding. Then we took two with us and started driving around town. We were arrested in the city center. The damage was six figures. Grass on golf courses, we found out, is expensive. We had destroyed the entire course. This became a local urban legend after that.

One summer evening we stole a car, and drove to the house of a drug dealer we knew was in jail. We broke in and took his safe with us in the trunk of the car, planning to open it at home. On the high-way we were followed by police for thirty minutes. We thought we were busted, but they were just behind us because they were going the same way. When the cops left, we dumped the safe on the side of the road, put the car back in the same place, went home and went to sleep.

We slept during the day and caused trouble at night. Being arrest-ed and staying a few nights at the police station in a cell was very normal to us. We did not even see this as a problem. It was a part of everyday life.

My mom cried a lot during this period; that did bother me, although I couldn't really figure out what she was so upset about. She told me once that she was happy each time she received a phone call from the police, telling her I'd been arrested and was in jail. At least she knew where I was then, and that I wasn't in danger any more. The happiest times were when she knew they were keeping me there for a few nights in isolation for questioning. At least then she could stop worrying and get some sleep.

We did not use any drugs, not even once. I didn't smoke cigarettes, drink, or do anything. I even stopped smoking weed. Sober, non-stop. I really loved what I was doing, and did not want to cloud my mind. The excitement I got from our criminal adventures became my drug of choice.

# FIRST LESSON

I started fights with my old friends. I'd have huge arguments with Bas and Frank; especially with Bas, whose behavior started to annoy me. *Pussy, I thought, Doesn't even stick up for himself.* Everyone made fun of him behind his back, saying his father was gay, his mother was ugly, and his little sisters were retarded. He knew they did this, but he still called these people friends.

I hated this about him. But at the same time I hated those people as well. *Make up your mind. You're either friends, or you're not. Don't pretend to be someone's friend, and then as soon as his back is turned stick a knife in it.* What bothered me the most was that Bas accepted being treated this way, as long as they'd be friends with him to his face. It was pathetic.

We made fun of him and screwed with his head as much as we could. At least we were doing it to his face, not like those other two-faced assholes. Those people were worthless.

Once, Bas was drunk and we had a huge fight. Bas was taller, heavier, and stronger than me. He also had two arms. He got so angry he started beating me up using a skateboard as a baseball bat. I limped away while all who witnessed it laughed. Alvin and I went to Bas's house that night. We broke in and messed up the place, stole his phone, and drank all the Coke out of his fridge.

He knew it was us and reported it to the police. I got arrested for it, but he dropped the charges.

Bas called me on the phone, 'Mark, if you would just use all that energy and creativity you have for something positive, you might get very far in life. Now, you are only fucking things up for yourself. Get a life, man!'

If I'd listened, my life may have been a whole lot easier.

As it was, I didn't listen. At seventeen, I ended up in court, I'd been arrested for: Destruction of property, grand theft auto, burglary.

On top of that, the prosecutor had a whole list of unsolved crimes in which they were searching for a young white man with one arm in the area around Zwolle. There was no way I was bullshitting my way out of that.

All the while, I was still thinking other people were doing this to me. I still felt like that little kid who moved from the big city to be handed over to the offspring of local rednecks. I was merely defending myself. I was scared.

The verdict was nine months, but my lawyer got me a deal: three months of supervision by parole officers and psychologists, and daily therapy to understand why I was in this situation and learn how to stay out of trouble. How I would spend the remaining six months would be determined based on the results from these sessions.

There I was; inside, angry at the world, and blaming everyone else for my situation. My fellow inmates were stupid idiots, but the parole officers were actually quite nice. They were usually in a good mood, and didn't put too much pressure on me. While I was inside, I also met Aldo, a parole officer who had a huge influence on my life, even if he didn't realize it.

Aldo took a liking to me from the beginning. He was middle aged, short, with black hair and a big nose. He told me he was Greek; his family moved to the Netherlands from Greece when he was little. Somehow, he was able to see through me, beneath the veneer of bullshit and attitude, and saw what kind of person I really was. He felt I had no business being in there. I was just struggling.

Aldo helped me see the world from a different perspective. He was the first one to tell me that even though I felt I was forced to do things I didn't want to do; I was still the one in control. I didn't have to do any of those things, but whatever I chose would have consequences, so I should choose wisely.

'Even when things piss you off,' he said, 'you don't have to react in a negative way. You can rise above, Mark. You're better than those people. You're better than that. You're smart. So why are you being so stupid?'

For a while, his words triggered a shift in my attitude, but I was still too stuck in my life experience, and it didn't bring lasting change. My life had to get much worse before any real lesson would be learned.

And much worse was coming.

When the three months were almost up, I had to appear in front of the judge again to determine how I would spend my remaining months. I sat in court, nervous again. My lawyer and parole officers pleaded that I was a smart and talented kid — if you looked through my anger and bad manners — who wanted to be a cartoonist.

The judge asked for a piece of paper, and had it brought to me.

'Draw something,' he said.

Everyone in the court room was staring at me. Minutes went by. Days. Fucking months. I started to sketch.

When the judge was handed the paper back, he held it up for everyone to see. I'd drawn a sexy cartoon character, and signed it with big, bold letters. The whole room laughed.

The judge had a surprise for me. There was a children's day-care center that needed their walls painted. They wanted me to do it, and while I was at it, paint the Looney Tunes characters on it. Half my time would be spent painting, and the other half picking up kids from school and helping out in other ways.

I had never worked with children, but I'd take it. It was better than prison. I painted the Looney Tunes characters on their walls and spent my remaining time playing board games with the kids. I made sandwiches, built Lego castles, and played basketball.

*Anything is better than prison.*

# FREEDOM

My sentence ended, and I was free. For the first time, I understood I was in control, and I was excited to be out. But now that I was on probation, I knew stealing cars wouldn't be smart and I grew bored.

To fill this void, I started using drugs, a lot of drugs. It began with an XTC pill, and I loved it. Next I tried amphetamines, and stayed awake for three nights in a row. Cocaine followed. I had done shrooms before, but I started doing them more often now. My favorite combination was shrooms and cocaine — and weed of course. There was always weed. I loved it when the mushroom trip was going strong and the whole world was moving and colorful. Then I'd take a big fat line of cocaine, and it was colored sparkles that shot through my brain and into my eyes.

It was spectacular. In Zwolle, it was all there was to do, really. It's either drugs or boredom.

I took twenty-five XTC pills in one day once because I kept forgetting I took some already, I had lost count. While I was out on my bike getting more weed, I realized how many I took, and panicked. I rushed home, and tried to puke them out. But nothing came.

I became sick. Really sick. I spent the whole week in bed. When I went to the doctor's office, he gave me a full physical.

'Mark, I gotta tell you, the results of your tests.... you're in better physical condition than eighty percent of my patients.'

'You gotta be shitting me, Doc. I feel fucking terrible; I'm scared I might die.'

'You won't die. Stop making all that drama. Go home, get some rest, drink some orange juice. You're in perfect shape!'

*Why didn't he lie to me? Why didn't he just lie?*

I got little jobs here and there, painting cartoon characters on walls for kids and designing logos for local businesses to make ends meet. I made some money with it and was able to support myself while still living with my mom.

A national newspaper created a platform for young and upcoming artists to publish their work, without pay of course. I sent in a whole truckload of my work. It must have been over one hundred comics I had written and drawn. They found four of them good enough to publish.

From that moment on, I told every magazine I spoke to that my comics were nationally published. It got me more assignments for big magazines, and, finally, I felt I was on my way.

*Foxy,* a new adult magazine, had become bigger than *Playboy* (in the Netherlands anyway) by focusing on amateur porn made with local girls. I heard they were looking for two new comic artists to publish on two pages in their monthly magazine.

One night I stayed up all night using speed, weed, and alcohol, and came up with the most distasteful, sexually graphic, and childish comic the country had ever seen. It was about a granny having anal sex with Santa Claus and his reindeers. Exactly the type of shit my mind came up with while on speed. They absolutely loved it, and gave me the full two pages for my own. They published my work for two years.

It felt so cool, and I was proud, but the money was not that great yet. If I made minimum wage doing this, I considered it lucky. Artists were a dime a dozen. It was very hard to get a good price for your work.

I still felt that the way for me to make real money would have to be something illegal. That was all I knew. It's stupid how the human mind can be trapped in an old way of thinking.

*Why are you being so stupid?*

# AMY

Iran out of speed at 3:00 am. I'd been working on a comic book all night, but with nothing left to fuel me, there were only two options. Try to get some sleep, or score one more gram and pull an all-nighter. I knew sleep was impossible.

I drove my dented green car to a friend's house. He was a dealer, and I was sure he'd still be awake. He lived in a tiny house on the corner of a small street in one of the worst neighborhoods in town. His house was always a mess. There were people coming and going throughout the night, people like me, people that wanted drugs. It was my best bet.

I rang the doorbell and a bald-headed man wearing a black jacket and ripped jeans opened the door.

'Wassup?'

'sup?' I answered.

I walked through the tiny, littered hallway and into the living room on the right. It smelled sweaty and musty inside, as if it had been slept in all night. There was a fat guy wearing sunglasses sitting in a chair, watching a tall black man cut lines of speed with his credit card on a little mirror placed on top of the TV. I walked over and asked for a line.

'Go right ahead,' he said while giving me a small metal straw to snort with.

There were more men standing around the room, chewing gum intensely. One guy was sitting on the floor reading CD album covers, surrounded by weed, tobacco, and rolling papers.

I was surprised to find a girl in the room, in the middle of all these pale looking men, sniffing lines from a glass plate on the table.

I wouldn't describe her as pretty, but she had a certain undeniable sex appeal. She wore baggy clothes, and her dyed-red hair was stuffed beneath a green Che Guevara baseball cap.

She was a little bit chubby, with dark brown eyes, and when she smiled two large front teeth appeared, making her look like an adorable hamster, on drugs.

'Hey, I'm Mark,' I said, trying not to sound nervous.

'Hey, I'm Amy.'

I sat down next to her on the sofa. Amy's pupils were dilated. She had little chunks of white powder on the edges of both nostrils. I had never met such a girl, especially not around the types of people I spent my time with. *How did she end up here?*

Amy told me she was in her final year of high school. She just turned eighteen. After graduation, she wanted to go to Bolivia to do volunteer work, before starting university in Amsterdam.

'What are you planning on studying?' I asked.

'I haven't decided yet, I would like to pursue a career in politics so that's something to keep in mind. But for now I am only thinking of finishing high school and going over to South America. I know I can do a lot of good there. There are many people that need our help.' She had a twinkle in her eye as she said it. She leaned over to suck another line up her nose through a rolled up ten-euro bill.

Amy's long front teeth prevented her from correctly pronouncing the letter R in some words. One of those words happened to be my name. She called me 'Madek'.

I found her to be a warm, endearing person. She seemed smart as well, compared to the idiots I was usually around. After an hour, I offered her a ride home. She took a few big sips from a half empty two liter bottle of Sprite, let out a three-second long burp while she turned the cap back on it, smiled and accepted.

*Fucking adorable.*

We sat in my car in front of her parents' house, and watched the sun peak over the horizon.

'Ok, so thank you for the ride,' she said. 'It was nice to meet you.'

She looked in my eyes, then at the ground, then back in my eyes again.

'So, are we gonna make out, or what?' I asked her.

I surprised myself. Normally I wouldn't be this bold with girls, but with Amy I had an instinct telling me that I could. The way she looked at me, she gave me a feeling as if she told me to move forward. I did it on autopilot.

She looked at me surprised, 'wow, you have some balls.'

'I know, come here!' I tried to grab her.

'No! I can't, I have a boyfriend.' She pushed me away.

I looked her in her eyes and smiled, 'so, dump him then... you know I'm better.'

I had no idea who this guy was, or if I was better. It was the same instinct telling me to push forward. Her jaw dropped.

'Madek, you crazy! So you are saying that I should just dump my boyfriend that I have been with for over a year, for you?'

She leaned back and gave me a questionable look, but I could see she was a bit flattered as well. I looked at her with my most serious face, 'Yeah.'

She shook her head and smiled, 'No way! You are insane, that's not gonna happen!'

'Ok, well, it was nice meeting you anyway, I'm going, bye.'

I leaned into her with a finger pointing at my cheek, suggesting she should kiss me goodbye.

She came in closer, slowly. I turned my head slightly so that our cheeks were next to each other, and held it there. I felt her breath on my neck, and knew she felt mine. My nose touched her face just below her ear, while my lips grazed her cheek. I slowly placed the palm of my hand on her leg and I moved my lips toward hers. We kissed for the first time.

I felt she was enjoying it a lot. She opened the car door, and walked away, I followed her with my gaze, wondering why she was leaving. She stopped. In her hand she held her keys and looked at me.

'Are you coming, or what?'

We spent the new day together. Neither of us slept. When I was about to leave the next evening, she looked at me with a grin, and slightly shook her head.

'You....'

'Me?' I asked, giving her my most innocent look.

'You are a piece of work!'

The following week she dumped her boyfriend, and we were dating. I cared about Amy a lot. To me, she represented an innocence that I had to protect in the middle of all these junkies, dealers, and criminals.

# SELLING WEED

We — Alvin and I — wanted to be rich or famous, but preferably both. The only famous people we knew were in a local rap group that went to our high school. The only rich people we knew were our drug dealers.

I still wanted to make it in the world as a big time cartoonist, but until that happened, I'd do what I needed to make money: sell weed. I sure smoked enough of it, so I could probably sell it, I thought.

Selling weed in the Netherlands is legal, as long as you have a license and are the owner of a hash bar. It's illegal to grow in large quantities, and it's illegal to sell it if you don't have a license. I didn't have a license. But I did know a guy named Bernie. Bernie was always in the park, smoking weed and drinking beer.

He was way older than us, well over forty. His sons, who also smoked weed, were our age. Bernie's whole family smoked weed nonstop—father, mother, and two sons—and you could tell just by their appearance. Bernie was pale and skinny, with bags beneath his eyes and a hideous mustache above his lips.

What his wife lacked in facial hair she made up for with wrinkles. Her face was covered in them, wrinkles on top of wrinkles, like someone had taken an eighty-year-old face and pasted it to her head. Their clothes were old and dirty, and never fit right.

One of his sons was also called Bernie. I called him little Bernie. It was a tradition in their family to give the first born son that name. Little Bernie wore baggy pants, a baseball cap, and always a T-shirt with some cartoon character on it.

His other son, Michael, never stopped talking. He was always bugging everyone to get more weed. I spent all my days with them for over a year, smoking weed every day. Especially Michael. I saw him all the time. He really did nothing other than hang out with his dad and smoke weed.

Bernie was stoned 24/7. If you got to his house at nine in the morning, he'd already be stoned for a few hours. If you spent a day with him in the same room, you'd be stoned just from the second-hand smoke.

He had big stories about his past, and I was eager to believe them.

'I used to be rich,' he said. 'Owned the biggest weed plantation in the province.'

'The oldest hash bar in town used to belong to me,' he said.

'Someone tried to shoot me in the head once, but I hit the gun out of his hand just in time,' he said, turning his ear toward me so I could see the scar the bullet had left.

'Bernie,' I asked, 'why don't you use some of your contacts to get me some top notch weed, for a better price. I'm tired of making these hash bars rich. Get me half a kilo of top- quality weed. Prove to me you're not bullshitting us all this time.'

'Dude, me bullshitting? You just wait! I'll get you your weed, no problem! Who do you think I am? You'll have your weed, you can be sure of that!'

He was nodding and curling his mouth in an attempt to look serious as he spoke. 'You just wait!'

The next day, there it was: five hundred grams of Silver Haze. It was exceptional weed. Green with a white layer of tiny THC crystals shimmering in the sunlight. I was stoned for months.

Alvin and I got dollar signs in our eyes. We thought Bernie was our ticket to becoming successful weed dealers. He had all the contacts, and we had money. *What could go wrong?*

The three of us decided to go into business. We bought and sold multiple kilos of weed every week. He got us fifteen kilos of hash that we would start transporting to other countries like Germany and the UK. But Bernie seemed to be more interested in smoking it himself than actually making a profit.

We also discovered a few holes in his storylines and realized the facts didn't add up. We asked some of the people from his stories about it, but they did not confirm any of it. Or they told us their side of the story, which was way less glamorous than Bernie made it seem. He apparently shot himself in the ear when he was playing with a gun. He was lucky he didn't blow his own head off.

I grew sick of Bernie's bullshit, and of his weed-induced mood swings as well.

'God fucking dammit, who smoked the last bit of weed I had lying here?' he screamed through the room.

'Yeah I did, that's all I've had today!' Michael replied.

'Fucking piece of shit! Now what am I supposed to smoke? Mark! Hand me that brick of hash from the closet over there, I'll just smoke that then!'

I looked at the brick of hash. I looked back at Bernie.

'No man, fuck that, no. That's our merchandise. We're supposed to make a profit here. What are you doing?'

'Ah, we'll make a profit, don't you worry. Hand it over!'

'No, fuck you man, no! I invested my money in this, and you're just going to smoke it like that?'

He looked at me with eyes that shot fire. 'What did you say? You invested YOUR money? I invested my time, efforts, and contacts!'

'Ah fuck off Bernie, your contacts think you're an idiot. I invested my money, this is my product, and you are not smoking it!'

Bernie reached over to the table next to his chair. He opened a drawer, and took out a switchblade. 'What did you say to me?'

'What are you gonna do with that? What? Are you gonna kill me? Don't make me laugh.' I stood up in front of him with my chest forward. I was pissed.

'I'm so fucking sick and tired of this shit,' I continued. I walked over to the closet where the rest of the hash was stashed.

'Just leave me the fuck alone, I'm leaving this shit hole!'

I threw the 15 bricks of hash in a bag, turned around, and found Bernie standing in front of me pointing his knife at my stomach.

'I will kill you, your motherfucker!' He was right up in my face with his eyebrows frowned. I looked down at the knife, and looked to the side to find a way to get out. Michael was blocking the exit. I was stuck.

'Really, Bernie? Really? Ok, just fucking do it then. If this is worth going to prison over for you, just fucking stab me then. Go ahead!'

I was shaking. We stared at each other for a few seconds.

'So, what are you gonna do?'

He threw the knife on the floor. I pushed him aside and walked to the front door. Michael tried to block my way. 'Let him go, son!' Bernie said. Michael stepped aside.

I threw the hash in the trunk of my car, and drove off.

I never saw Bernie again.

# WE HEARD YOU HAVE 15 KILOS

Now I was stuck with an excessive amount of product, poor connections in the business, and money problems. Alvin told me not to worry. He had my back. We were gonna do this together. I was happy I had a friend like him.

Word got out on the streets that I had fifteen kilos of hash, and that I was now in business on my own. I tried to avoid the people in this business and sold what I had per gram to anyone who would buy. I was trying to get my money back ten euros at a time.

I sold weed and hash all day. I even bought a kilo of amphetamines and started selling that. Sometimes a client wouldn't pay and I'd have to resort to violence.

After Alvin and I beat someone up for not paying me 10 bucks that he owed, he called me on the phone.

'Mark! Fuck you man! You only beat me because Alvin was there! If it was just you and me I'd kick your ass because you only have one arm! Let's meet up now and fight!'

'Dude, I'm a hundred percent sure you'd beat me in a fight. I really don't care. I'm not trying to prove who is stronger here. You just need to pay me and that's it. If you really want to fight I can send someone over to kick your ass again, but I am really not gonna move. I already put in way more effort than this shit is worth to me. Now if you waste my time even more I'll really get pissed off. Just get me my money!'

All this trouble over this little cash. But I'd have to do it, or I might as well quit. It was a terrible way to live. I hated it. I really hated it. This was no life for me.

*I wanted to be a cartoonist. I'm a creative, soft hearted person. What the fuck happened?* I'd say to myself then, what I'd say to you now; *you're better than that. You're smart. So why are you being so stupid?*

Between these shady deals, I worked on my art. I wrote stories, drew cartoons and comics, sprayed graffiti. I read science and philosophy books. I played chess. Those were the things I really enjoyed doing.

One evening, Amy and I were at my mom's house, stoned as fuck. My mom was not home that weekend. The bell rang. I didn't open because I didn't feel like it. I was so high and enjoying myself, I wanted the whole world to just leave me alone. It rang again, and again, and again. It kept ringing for minutes at a time. Then, a series of loud bangs like someone was trying to break the door down. I told Amy to stay quiet, then put on some clothes and went downstairs to look.

I peeked through the window, and saw two Moroccan guys from the neighborhood. They were well-known drug dealers. One was tall, with broad shoulders and a belly bulging beneath his T-shirt. A long scar covered the side of his face, splitting several days of unshaven stubble in half. The other man was short, clean shaven and dressed well. Despite their different appearance, one thing was obvious: both men were high. Their wide-open eyes and dilated pupils meant cocaine, speed, or both.

I opened the door. *Why did I open the door?*

'Oh, so you ARE home!' they said. 'Can we come in?' It was not a question.

'No man, rather not right now, it's not a good time, can you come back later?' I was in no mood for this shit.

'Later? Why later? We are here now. Why come back later? I don't see the point.' the taller man replied.

'Man, listen, I'm with a girl... This is not a good time.'

'Hahaha! Mark has got some bitch upstairs! Hehehe, nice work, player! We'll only be a minute. Don't worry,' they said, shoving me aside and walking in.

'We've heard you're selling hash. Can we buy some from you?' They looked at each other and grinned.

'No, I'm not selling. I don't have any. Maybe next time, ok?'

The shorter man pulled out a knife and pointed it at me. 'We heard you have fifteen kilos. Where is it?'

'I don't have any,' I said. 'What makes you think I...' I never finished the question. The man with the knife lunged toward me, slamming his fist into my stomach before I could react, a sledgehammer pounding into my flesh. I doubled over and he lifted me up, pushed me against the wall, and held the knife against my throat. He pressed it hard enough to pierce the skin. I looked in his deep, crazed eyes, and thought about Amy. Upstairs. What will they do to her? I could never forgive myself if they hurt her. I needed to get them out.

'I've got some,' I said. 'A little. You can have it.' He loosened his grip and took a small step back. I walked to a place I'd stashed one kilo, separate from the rest, and held it out to him.

'That's all I have.'

He looked at the brick of hash as if it was more than he had ever seen. That surprised me.

The tall one said I should be scared. This guy just got released from a mental institution and he'd kill me if I didn't cooperate. I'm not sure if that was true, but it didn't matter. I was scared anyway. They searched the house and found some money, then left.

I grabbed the rest of the hash and went with Amy to her house. I called up Alvin and told him what had happened.

'Well, dude,' he stammered, 'Uhh… what do you expect of me? I mean these guys are not something to fuck with…'

*Oh, I thought you had my back, what happened to that? Mother-fucker.* I hung up the phone.

I was alone, again. *So much for that brotherhood.*

# REGULAR PEOPLE

I slipped into a severe depression. I tried to numb it with weed, but it only made it worse. I had failed as a cartoonist. I didn't make enough money, and I wasn't famous. I had failed as a dealer. It only cost me money and gave me problems. The person I thought had my back, didn't. I felt alone, betrayed, and stupid.

I sat inside all day, stoned from smoking the strongest weed I could get. A gram and a half of amphetamines disappeared up my right nostril every twenty-four hours. There was a kilo laying around, so no shortage of that. I no longer showered, brushed my teeth, or even bothered getting out of bed. This went on for weeks. My thoughts were plagued by memories of all the choices I had made, and the stupid shit I had done that led me here. I thought about the bullies in school, when I'd just moved to Zwolle.

I remembered the teachers that always took the bullies' side. I remembered my anger and lust for revenge on the simpleminded people in this stupid fucking town. I remembered the things my parole officer, Aldo, told me about choices and options. I looked out the window and saw the neighbors just living their lives, doing normal things, not having a clue of the kind of problems I had created for myself. I was jealous of those people. For the first time, I felt they were smarter than I was.

*Who's the fucking stupid one now?*

Other people in the business told me to get back at them. Get a baseball bat and hurt them. I was even advised to purchase a gun and shoot them, to really scare them or, even better, kill them. The truth is, I didn't plan on doing anything. It just wasn't worth it to me. These guys apparently got excited by one measly kilo of hash.

45

All the violence, all the risk, for what? One stupid kilo? One kilo was nothing, definitely not worth these problems.

But to them it was. In this business, if someone steals even one cent from you, you have to strike them back hard, violently, or everyone will walk all over you. All this trouble for something so small. The voices telling me to take revenge and resort to violence sounded more and more ignorant to me. I was surrounded by idiots.

I was not going to make the situation worse than it already was. I realized something — a realization that just came to me after all these problems and headaches.

Suddenly everything was crystal clear, bright as day.

*Regular people don't have this problem.*

*Regular, normal, everyday people, who have jobs and live normal lives, never have these problems. No one puts a knife to their throats. No one robs them of a kilo of hash.*

*They don't worry about their girlfriend upstairs, hiding in a closet, or beside the bed. These are problems I created. I made all the choices that led to this. If I had made different choices, this would not have happened.*

*It was my own fault. Being angry at them was useless. They did me a favor, if anything. I should actually thank them.*

*I could choose to be a criminal, and get thrown back in jail, or have to deal with other criminals like these guys. I could choose to take revenge on them and continue on the same path, most likely making the situation worse in the long run.*

*Or I could choose not to.*

*I need to get the fuck away from this place.*

# PUSSY

People called me a pussy for not doing anything, for not taking my revenge. But it was very clear to me that just letting them live their lives was revenge enough. They'd screw up their lives even more if I'd just let them be.

I'd be fighting an enemy that had nothing to lose. That was a battle I couldn't win. They would be willing to resort to way more violence for less money than I would. It was way too much hassle, with nothing to win.

I still wanted to become a famous cartoonist, and I was not gonna let that be screwed up by a couple of low lives. I tried to explain to a friend why I decided not to do anything.

'Listen, if you look at it, it's my own fault, isn't it?'

'What do you mean? They are the ones who came to your house and robbed you, so it's their fault, isn't it?' he replied.

'But I led those type of people into my life, right? I was in charge of that. The moment it started going wrong was the moment I decided to go into this business. I created this by spending my time with junkies, drug dealers, and criminals. I've invited this into my life.'

He looked at me like I was speaking Chinese. 'Huh? Well you just think about this way too much. You shouldn't do that.'

The words 'way too much' could have been left out of that statement. He should have said I thought about it. That's it. It wasn't too much thinking. It was just thinking.

'I'll talk to you in ten years, and then we'll see who was right.' I replied.

I realized I was the one who screwed up my life. I fucked up, and I could make it better. I didn't know what to do, I just knew I had to stop doing what caused these problems for me. The more I thought about it, the more I understood why I was behaving that way. I was trying to get back at the town for treating me so badly when I moved there. I was also trying to keep people at a distance because I was scared. I hated the teachers, the police, and everyone for being un-fair and mean to me when I was a child.

Anger was a decision. It's like a drug I was addicted to. It's a feeling I was holding onto. I could choose to let it go. But, like any addict, I was not admitting this to myself. It was stronger than I was, I thought. But it wasn't. I was the one keeping this anger alive. This whole time, anger was my drug of choice.

I held on to my anger because it gave me the feeling of having my revenge on them. But what I was doing now was not hurting them at all. That time was gone. Those people were gone. Everything I was doing now, I was doing to myself. I was taking revenge on myself, and I didn't think I deserved that.

I did not want to see Alvin again either. He just didn't bring me anything good. Sure, we both hated Zwolle. Sure, we had similar negative experiences and reacted in a similarly negative way. But I didn't want to focus on negativity. I saw where that got me.

Relationships based on negativity should be avoided. It's better to have nothing in common than something negative. He didn't take it well, but I told him to accept it. That brotherhood with him was some form of misplaced loyalty I did not have any longer.

That was the first time it hit me. People with the wrong intentions are stealing from you, even if they aren't literally taking money out of your pocket. Just being around these people will cost you — sometimes more than money can buy. The people you spend time with will influence you, whether you want them to or not.

Amy was still hanging out with horrible people. One day she went to some party with a bunch of dealers and junkies. I called her on the phone.

'Amy, please, don't go with them. Be smart, these people, you shouldn't spend your time with them. They pull you down to their level and want to keep you there, you are better than this!'

'I don't understand, nothing will happen! Come on, you know these guys! Madek, why don't you come with us?'

'Yes, I know them, I know they are junkies. I know they are idiots. I know that spending even one minute out of the year with them will cost you. Just don't go with them!'

'Oh, so now you suddenly feel you are better than they are? Madek, come on, what is the worst that can happen?'

'The worst that can happen? Everything that happens with these people is fucking terrible! I just want to leave this life behind me, don't you get it? I can't do that if my girlfriend will still spend time with them. Come on, just be smart, don't go with them. Let's go do something else!' I pleaded with her.

'Oh, Willy wants to speak to you!' She replied, and handed the phone over to a guy named Willy. Willy was a hardcore drug user. I knew him through his older brother, who stayed in the same cell-block as me.

'Hey, Mark! How's it going, man?'

'What the fuck do you want, Willy?' I was pissed that Amy just handed him the phone like that, and pissed that he was wasting my time.

'Mark, come on, man, you have nothing to worry about. Just let her go, I'll be with her, I'll keep my eye on her, you have my word!'

*You'll be with her? You'll have your eye on her? Are you fucking serious? That's exactly the fucking problem, genius.*

I hung up the phone without saying anything. Another realization hit me. One that hurt me even deeper. Amy chose to be with these people. That was her choice, not mine. If she didn't see the same things as me, there was nothing I could do about it. As much as I wanted to protect her, she had her own free will. She couldn't even see what I was trying to protect her from.

I ended that relationship. It was negative as well. This was the toughest choice, but I knew it was the right one.

I was still worried about her a lot because of the people she chose to spend her time with. I pleaded with her to stop doing this. However, she turned this around and made it seem to everyone as if I wanted her to come back to me and that that's why I was so upset. When this became clear, I broke off all contact with her.

Years later, I heard from someone that she finally understood what I was trying to tell her.

She realized it after being raped. I was devastated.

# BARRY

The only person I still wanted to see was a young man named Barry. Barry bought drugs from me many times, that's how I knew him. He made me laugh and was always very friendly to me. He was more than a client. Barry told me he also started to hate the environment I was trying to escape.

Barry was a guy from an even tinier village near Zwolle. He had the manners and appearance of white trailer trash. He did, however, live in a regular house. He had blonde hair down to his shoulders, crooked yellow teeth, and dressed overly flashy, but only in the cheaper brands. He lacked a subtlety in his style, but I found that to be endearing. Barry and I smoked weed together and did cocaine.

The things Barry and I had in common were that we both had bad relationships with our fathers, and we both wanted to be rich. I think the main thing we had in common was our drug use though, but neither of us was ready to admit this at that time.

Barry was able to roll joints while driving his car. Nice joints, with real craftsmanship. They were the best. Barry spoke a lot too, and would rant while we smoked together.

'You know, Mark. My dad, he is a fucking piece of work.'

Barry inhaled deeply, making the cone shaped joint light up and shrink an inch. He exhaled a big cloud of smoke through his mouth and nose.

'Once, when I was a little kid, I don't remember exactly how old, I must have been around ten or eleven. I was visiting my dad with my brother. My dad, you know, he is very wealthy. I was lying on the back seat of his car. My brother was in the passenger seat, my dad drove. They thought I was sleeping, but I wasn't. I overheard my dad say to my brother that next time when he came to visit, he should leave me at home. He said I was gonna be a loser anyway. He said I'll be a junky, a street punk, good for nothing. I was just a little kid, how do you think that made me feel? My own father! I never told them I heard him say this.'

The corners of his mouth curled down, his eyebrows frowned, and he took another one of those long intense puffs from his joint.

'Fucking hell dude.' I replied, looking down at my feet.

'Yeah, fuck that guy.'

Barry took another big puff, before handing the joint to me.

I told him a story about when I was visiting my dad. After not being in touch for years, we reconnected and I visited him in Scotland, where he had moved. He lived there with his third wife. He left the other woman in Zwolle in a similar drastic way, and had now remarried an English woman. I stayed at his house alone, and couldn't find him for days. I tried to reach his phone but he wasn't picking up. Then I got a call from his wife saying that they were in the Netherlands, and they would be back the week after. Not even from him personally, but from his wife. Like he didn't care.

It turned out that he was very close to my sisters in Zwolle. When he returned I asked him if he went to visit them and the grandkids he never saw.

'No, and don't tell them that we were there,' was his reply. Barry and I shared many stories like this, while doing lots of drugs and fantasizing about becoming rich and having everything we wanted.

Barry was a direct marketer, meaning he would stop people in the street and sell them subscriptions to newspapers and things like that. He was pretty slick. He could make you feel like he was your best friend if he wanted to.

I was warned about him by several people. They were saying he would always find a way to pay the least whenever there was a bill to split, and he would screw over his friends if it would get him ahead. When I asked him why people had that opinion about him, he said, 'Yeah, with those people, yes. But never with you.' It gave me a feeling of sharing a brotherhood with Barry. 'We are like family, Mark.'

He was like family.

# THE WORST KIND OF PEOPLE

The negative people I knew could have been the junkies and drug dealers, who of course were bad. Alvin also might have been a bad guy, although I knew deep down he really wasn't, just like I really wasn't. But the worst people were actually the ones in the middle — the regular people who didn't really do anything bad but did nothing good either.

Those people were not moving forward or backward. They were just standing still. It's the vast majority of the population. Before I knew I had more options, I always felt as if those people were the ones who drove me toward the negative. At least the negative people were doing something, anything.

I just needed something in my life to do, something to work on, and the only option that was presented to me was the negative option. It was either that or do nothing, I thought. I didn't realize I had a few more choices.

The people in the middle, the people who did nothing, were the same type as the kids in school who would surround the bully that picks on the weakest kid and laugh. Or they'd just stand there and look. They are actually the culprits, not the bully. The bully is a victim of them as well because those people make him feel as if he is being 'cool' while he is actually fucking up his own life as well.

I always felt they even rewarded the bully for his behavior, which is why I became one myself. The bully has his own problems — his own fear of not fitting in — and that group of people make him feel as if that is his way of being accepted by them. If I really looked at it, my criminal behavior was born out of the same fear that was created when I got bullied in school.

The people who do nothing are the worst. They facilitate the bad things that happen. I'm not sure if they are too dumb, too weak, too scared, or they literally don't care about anyone but themselves. Whatever it was, I was so sick of it. People without opinions, people without courage, people who put in no effort whatsoever to better their lives or the lives of others were the type of people I had seen way more of than I should. I was so incredibly sick of them, even more than the junkies and drug dealers.

I had involuntarily built up a pretty bad reputation in this town. I knew I wanted to change my life, and with that, my reputation. But I hated the people I knew in Zwolle, nonetheless. My reputation and history in the town didn't even matter. Setting aside any bad emotions from the past, these were just not my kind of people. They were too small-minded and had too few aspirations.

I could of course put in a lot of work and effort to better my reputation there. *But for what?*

After I'd put in all that effort, I would still be in Zwolle surrounded by these same idiots who sparked this type of behavior in me in the first place. It wouldn't do me any good. *What would be my prize? What would be the reward?*

Nothing. I would gain literally nothing by doing that. I'd be back where I started, and I hated where I started. That was the problem to begin with. That was the whole point, the whole reason why everything went to shit. *Why go back to that?*

It was better to just go to an environment where I wanted to be, with people I actually liked, and just start from scratch. It would be way more effective and make me way happier.

Teachers in school prevented me from having dreams. That's why I hated school. I loved learning, but I hated school. In school they prevented me from learning anything except what they wanted me to learn. What they wanted me to learn was that I should be part of those people in the middle. But those people were horrible, and I'd rather be a bad person than be one of them — if those were my only two options. People I grew up around wanted me to act normal and be realistic. But this was not realistic at all. This was horrible. This was a trap I needed to get out of.

When I was a kid, I accepted the world in the way it was presented to me by grownups, but I knew now that I could create my own world. I had created a terrible world for myself, but make no mistake, I was the one that created it. The world was bigger than what I'd seen so far. It was bigger than my environment tried to force me to believe it was — way bigger.

There were many more options than the two presented to me by small-minded people. Any of those options would present me with a whole new set of options. The options in life are endless — good or bad. This is something these people would never understand.

# A DIFFERENT STATE
# OF MIND

After being robbed by drug dealers, I broke contact with almost everyone, including Amy. However, dropping bad habits doesn't happen overnight.

I was chilling in Barry's car, on shrooms and coke. He was only on coke. While rolling a joint, Barry asked me, 'hey man, have you ever been to Poland?'

'No, why?'

He licked the rolling papers edge and rolled it shut.

'Man, it's only a 500-mile drive. We can easily do it in one day.'

'Yeah?'

'Dude, I hear Polish women are fucking gorgeous! I always wanted to go check it out. Why don't we just start driving now? We'll be there in 12 hours.'

I was now single, so the promise of fucking gorgeous women motivated me a lot.

'Fuck yeah, I'm not doing anything anyway...'

We loaded up on more weed and coke and started driving. Barry was only using cocaine, so he was still OK to drive. Halfway there,

58

my shrooms wore off, and we realized we had no idea what city we were going to.

We decided to call a friend who had been there before. He told us the closest and nicest city we could go to would be Poznan. When we arrived at that city, it looked different from any city I had ever seen. Buildings in Poznan were either old and in decay, or brand new with state of the art technology and design.

Poznan had a square in the center that was surrounded on all four sides by restaurants and clubs. A big cathedral stood in the middle. There were many people out there from all countries of the world. But most importantly for me at the time, there were women. So many women. None of which knew my history and what kind of person I used to be.

Everywhere you looked there were blonde or black haired girls walking in groups. They were all dressed up in stylish and sexy dresses, wearing high heels, on their way to the many night clubs in the city. They smiled at us as they passed.

We checked into a fancy hotel, ate in restaurants, partied in clubs, and did all the things we could not afford back in the Netherlands. In Poland it was all so cheap! In the Netherlands, everyone was under the impression that Polish people had a hard life, but from what I experienced, that was not the case at all. Poland was a lot of fun and surprisingly modern.

One club we went to looked like it was about to fall down from the outside. There were cracks in the walls, and a broken window with a wooden board nailed in front of it.

When we entered, it was one of the most amazing venues we'd ever seen. There were half naked girls dancing in cages, there were lasers dancing around to the rhythm of the music. The dance floor was packed with the most beautiful women I had ever seen, with the DJ spinning music high above them.

Another Club we went to was in the basement of a brand new shopping mall that was designed as an old factory mixed with the newest architecture. They flew in a DJ from the United States, so it was a hassle getting inside. The line was huge.

'Hey guys, where are you from?' I heard a lady's voice ask us. It was a short blonde haired girl with bright green eyes, wearing a black dress. She stood in front of a door, holding a key, in high black stilettos.

'We are from Holland, we just arrived,' I answered.

'Oh you guys wanna get inside? Yeah it's very crowded, wait I'll get you guys in.' She replied. She opened the door she was standing in front of, disappeared for 10 minutes, came back out, and held it open for us.

'Quickly, go inside!'

The club was amazing. People there were so friendly and helpful. This was so far out of my reality, different from anything I had ever experienced.

In my head, I imagined the world based on the experiences I'd had and the people I had known. But this experience, and these people, were from another world. They were so nice. Life there was fantastic. The way I felt, every inch of anger and frustration was just gone. It left my body. Nothing from back home mattered here. I felt wonderful. I'd driven ten hours, and I was in a completely different state of mind.

I returned to Zwolle, but my mind stayed in Poznan.

# A GOOD MOVE

Roan was a kid that hung out with the same group of lowlifes I spent my time with in Zwolle. I knew him because we handed each other a joint every once in awhile. He moved to Zwolle from a little village nearby, and lived with his mom in a horrible neighborhood. I used to dislike Roan a lot. He got on my nerves so much with his socially awkward behavior.

Roan was very skinny. He always had a surprised look on his face, as if he had no clue what was going on around him, and never belonged anywhere. You know how in high school you have those kids that just get on your nerves? They aren't really doing anything wrong, but you just can't stand them. These kids are usually bully-magnets. That was Roan. He was one of those kids.

His jeans were always too small, and his T-shirts were more holes than fabric. He had short, brown hair on his tiny head and moved awkwardly on his long and skinny legs, letting his arms swing a bit too much back and forth as he walked.

He was weird and annoying, but he knew a lot about computers and building websites, and I needed a website when my comics were nationally published. Roan agreed to make a website for me. We spent a lot of time together on this project, and I discovered that I actually liked him a lot. He was very smart and funny in an inappropriate way, exactly the type of humor I found hilarious. After working on my website, we became friends. First impressions are deceiving.

I told Roan about Poznan, and he wanted to go check it out with me. Three weeks later, we went there by bus.

The second time I was in Poznan, we connected with several locals and really built a group of friends. They got us a gram of amphetamines, stronger than anything I had ever used back home. We only took half a gram each but were awake for three nights. We just couldn't get to sleep, no matter how hard we tried.

I liked Poznan so much, compared to Zwolle at least. Everything was cheaper. The people were great. They were ten times more positive than the negative assholes I grew up with in Zwolle.

The obvious thought came into my head.

*I could live here.*

I could choose to completely remove myself from a negative environment, and place myself in a positive one. It would be a simple choice, with massive consequences.

If I stayed in Zwolle, I would always be confronted with my old life, and there would always be a chance to be pulled back into it. In Poznan, I was a different person. I knew different people. I did different things. It was a no brainer; my life there was better. I would spend my money in Polish Zlotys, but I could still work for Dutch magazines, drawing cartoons and comics, who would pay me in euros.

Within one month I had gotten an apartment in the city center and moved to Poznan. I sold the remaining twelve kilos of Hash for fifty cents a gram to a local dealer. He looked at me like I was crazy. Just over half a kilo of amphetamines was left after what I sold and used myself. I flushed it down the toilet.

I just wanted to be done with it. I wanted no more drug money. To me these weren't 'profits' any longer. Any money made in that dirty business was a loss for everyone involved. All I wanted was to leave. When I went to Poland, I just felt it in my entire body that this was a way to get out. I had an image in my head of being in a prison, and the door was wide open. I saw myself running to the door to get out while I could. I didn't care what I left behind. I just needed to leave.

In Zwolle, everyone said I was being stupid. To them, Poland was a poor country, and everyone in Poland wanted to live in the Netherlands. So why would I move there?

'If Poland is that great, then why are all Poles coming over here?' they said. All of the Polish people they had ever seen were construction workers who happened to get a job in the Netherlands because it paid better. To them, those were all the Polish people in the world.

Obviously this was in no way representative of the Polish population and culture. Those people, just like me, created their view of the world based on their own experiences. That view of the world was incorrect.

I knew I had made the right decision. I needed to get out of Zwolle, away from those people with their negative mind-sets who were pulling me down. Every person I had ever met had the same limited mind as the regular everyday people you'd meet in Zwolle. I thought the whole world was like Zwolle. I thought the whole world was stupid. But now I knew that wasn't the case.

My life had been terrible, and I knew how I got there. I had made it terrible, by my choices and my behavior. So my choice now was to do whatever it took not to make the same mistakes.

It's not that my hometown itself is a more negative place than any other. It's all what you make of it. It's not the location. It's the choices you make, the people around you and the effect they have on you.

I got pushed into a corner where I tried to hide from the world because I had learned that the world was hostile, violent, and scary. But it's not. It's what you make of it. If you want change, you'll have to create it. If you are in a bad environment, you'll have to get out of it. No one can do that but you.

It might be scary, but staying in the same place with the wrong people who keep you spiraling down is even scarier. I was afraid, but I told myself I would do it, even when afraid.

# CHOICES

When I moved to another country, it was my chance to do things differently. I could start over, and I knew exactly what I did not want. I was able to rebuild a social circle with the knowledge I had gained from my previous mistakes. I'd hand pick my friends. I'd only allow people in who were educated, intelligent, and positive — people who were doing something with their lives and gave me the feeling they were moving forward.

Bartek was the first guy we'd met. He was a bartender in one of the restaurants in the town square where Roan and I had dinner once. When he found out we were from Holland, he asked, 'oh, you guys smoke weed?' Bartek always smiled, and when he did, his eyes squinted beneath his glasses. He was an economy student at the university of Poznan. His father owned a huge co-packing company that he was going to be the manager of. He introduced us to a lot of other people.

There was Andrzej; he went by the nickname Gucio. Gucio was short and had a little belly. He dressed down to his underwear in brands like Hugo Boss, Versace, and Tommy Hilfiger. He studied international relations in university, but was also a DJ at all the main clubs and went by the DJ name Andy Mile. That was his passion. We could talk for hours about science, politics, and art, while smoking weed of course.

Then there was Anthony, I loved that guy. Blond spiky hair, round cheekbones, striped T-shirts. His nickname was Kura, which means chicken in Polish. I never found out why. Anthony was a genius. Gucio told me that one day in high school everyone took an IQ test. The next day some people came to school to announce that Anthony had a 175 IQ, which made him one of the smartest people on the planet. Like many of the people I met, Anthony smoked weed like a chimney, and was always in a good mood.

In Zwolle I always had the feeling I couldn't connect with anyone, because I had the feeling they were all dumb. In Poznan, I seemed to only meet smart people. I felt at home.

If people I spent time with influenced me no matter what, I was going to make sure they would influence me in a positive way. I actively denied people access if they showed any resemblance to the negative attitudes I had experienced before.

Using too many hard-drugs? Hanging out in the street? Not doing anything with your life? Sorry, but no, we can't be friends. I'm in charge of my own life. I was determined. Even the people in the middle, the ones who were not doing anything bad, but nothing good either, were not getting anywhere near my life. I didn't want it. I was so sick of it. I knew what I no longer wanted and would only be around people who made me be my best self.

All of this was having a remarkable effect on my morale and outlook on life. The way I dressed changed. I used to wear baggy pants and didn't really pay much attention to what I was wearing. I used to say that I didn't care about what I wore. But, if I didn't care, that would mean that I might as well be dressed in a suit and tie. It would be the same to me, right?

This actually meant I did care. I went clothes shopping with a female friend and asked her to help me pick out the right clothes and fit the right colors together.

My new choices in my social circle, behavior, and clothing gave me a whole new perspective on the world. The whole world was not hostile and stupid — only the people I knew back in Zwolle. It was the people I allowed into my life. I gave them access. It was my fault.

No one else was to blame. But just like my actions screwed it all up, my actions could save it as well.

There are actually a lot of great people in the world. You just have to go out and find them.

# PLEASANT MEMORIES

Whenever I went back to Zwolle, someone I knew had been to prison, died, or both. Two jumped off a building and died. One overdosed on god-knows-what and died in the middle of a field. Another literally drank himself to death. Another guy had psychosis after a bad LSD trip, and he roamed the streets homeless while mumbling to himself.

The story that stood out the most involved one guy I used to buy drugs from. We went to the same high school for a while, and spent time with the same friends. I heard he hung himself in prison after he was arrested for allegedly killing his own baby in a drugged-up rage.

I didn't know what to think of that. This was so insane, even for the kind of people I was used to already. It gave me the creeps, and I didn't want to think about it. I knew this baby. I had seen it many times. I also knew the mother. I was just happy I got out when I did, because things apparently took a turn for the worse after I'd left.

People from Zwolle wanted to visit me in Poznan, and asked for my number. I gave them a wrong one, so they couldn't reach me if they tried. A guy I used to know fell into depression and reached out to me for help. I blocked all his calls and emails. Someone gave me a call one day and said his friend had died, and he needed to talk. I never returned his phone call.

These were very tough decisions, but I knew then it was no one's responsibility but my own that my life was screwed up. So it was not my responsibility other peoples' lives were screwed up either. I had my hands full with my own problems and progress, and didn't need this distraction. *I'm sorry,* I thought, *but the guy you knew is gone. Please call someone else.*

This seems cold, but I needed to fix my own life before I could be there for someone else.

# OLD BUDDY

Every time I came back, I gave Barry a call, and we went through multiple grams of our favorite narcotics: cocaine and weed.

Somehow, back in Zwolle I would always fall back into old behavior. It had a power over me which I found hard to control. I read in psychology books later that our minds indeed link places to certain behavior and addictions.

Barry got a job at a massive direct sales company in Amsterdam. He was head of the department there. I was impressed. He showed me around the office, where he had 20 people working under him. The company paid for a luxurious hotel room that he stayed in most of the time.

One day, he quit and told me he was starting his own company. He rented an office space in the center of Zwolle and got four employees to go door-to-door selling subscriptions. The next time I arrived in Zwolle, he picked me up in a brand new Volkswagen convertible,

'Barry! Motherfucker! Great to see you man! How are you doing? How's business!? Nice looking car, man!' I shouted.

'Hehe... yeah man, business is going very well, very well...' He had one hand on the steering wheel, and in the other he held a joint between two fingers with his arm casually hanging over the car door. His crooked yellow teeth were visible, as he grinned from ear to ear.

He seemed so proud. It was funny to me. Barry was like a little kid I just wanted to see happy. When I saw that smile on his face, I just enjoyed it.

'Mark, I have plenty of guys working for me now, man. I will get more very soon. Business is booming! I got so many projects going on right now, I'm serious. Now is the time for me to take the risk and scrape in all the cash I can get my hands on!'

The next time I was in Zwolle, he was bankrupt.

His company never did as well as he made it seem, and that car was leased from the company revenue, while it was still at a loss. It was destined to fail. He was just keeping up appearances that whole time.

Barry was really in a tough spot financially. A job at a local employment agency was all he could get. Until he paid off his debt, that's what he would be doing.

Once Barry and I had a conversation about trees and plants in the car. I'm not sure how we got on that subject, but Barry was convinced that a tree was not a plant. I started laughing very loudly, and he got upset.

'Of course not! A tree is not a plant! A tree is, of course, something else than just a regular plant!' He shouted at me. I remember those words, 'just a regular plant.' I found it hilarious.

'Barry, listen.' I said, laughing hysterically. 'A tree is plant. I'm not sure what else I can tell you.'

'Of course not! From a tree you can make wood! From a plant you can't make wood!' He sounded really angry.

'Well, Barry, from a plant you actually can make wood because a tree is a plant. So all wood is made from plants.' I couldn't believe I was explaining this to a grown-up.

His facial expression changed, like he just had a realization. 'Oh, well, maybe you're right. Well, uh, I just didn't know that then.'

To me this was not something that was acceptable for a grown man not to know. If he'd been five years old, it would have been a different story. This still holds the record for the dumbest thing I've ever heard a grown man say.

# RICH CHARACTERS

In Poznan the people I met were rich — really, really rich. At least their parents were. I met an eighteen-year-old who drove a Jaguar. One kid's dad was one of the richest people in the country. His dad had a helicopter, an airplane, a fleet of luxury cars, and a couple of mansion- sized villas. He owned shopping malls and factories. This kid couldn't leave the house without a bodyguard. We were smoking weed at my place once, and his bodyguard was waiting outside my apartment like we were celebrities, or maybe gangsters.

In Poland it was not very common for people to speak English. German and Russian were taught as second languages in school, English not so much. On the TV, it was uncommon to have subtitles. In Poland they had their own kind of dubbing, so usually children didn't pick up English from the TV either, like they did in the Netherlands and Scandinavian countries.

I did not speak a word of Polish, and the only kids I could communicate with were the ones who'd been sent to private English schools by their parents. These happened to be the richer families in the city. Because of this, I automatically connected to the wealthier people in town.

In Poland, I was confronted with extreme wealth for the very first time. To this day, the richest people I know are Polish. Some of the guys from these extremely rich families are also some of the nicest people I know.

In Zwolle, I hung out with people from poor families, or middle class at most. Their attitude about rich people was quite negative. 'Those rich bastards,' was thrown around a lot when speaking of people with wealth. They thought rich people judged them for being poor, or that somehow these rich people made them poor.

Guess how many times my rich friends spoke hatefully about people because they had more, or less money? Absolutely zero. Never! It never happened. Of course, there was one guy from a rich family who was fat, ugly, and insecure. He felt better about himself because his parents were rich. But all the other rich kids laughed at him and said he was a loser.

This was just not acceptable and was viewed as being very low-value behavior. So who is judging people based on the amount of money they have? I realized, these kids could not help being born into a rich family, just like other kids could not help being born into a poor or middle class family. It makes no sense to judge people based on that. Judge people based on their character.

I also noticed a certain respect for money in these families. They were always trying to get the best deals, and weren't wasting food. Behavior is what matters. If someone is born rich or poor, it is not their fault. So don't judge them by it. No one controls this. Being born rich doesn't make you happy. Being born poor doesn't make you unhappy. This revelation paved the way for a change in mindset regarding money that I would have never gotten if I had stayed in Zwolle.

*A lot of poor people are poor because they have poor character, and a lot of rich people are rich because they have rich character.*

I spent a lot of time by myself in Poznan, because I didn't know that many people there. This was great, because it gave me time to work on my own behavior and read books about it. It also gave me all the time I needed to work on my comics that were still being published in magazines back home.

Amongst my favorite books were –

*How to Stop Worrying And Start Living,*

*How to Win Friends And Influence People,*

*The Secret.*

I read most of them several times. Self-improvement was my main focus. Self- improvement became my drug of choice. In a conversation with someone I knew back home, I mentioned these books and how much I was learning from them. The reaction was, 'Haha! You're reading books on how to make friends! Hahaha!' *Yes, laugh, you stupid idiot, we'll see.* These books all confirmed what I was already thinking.

*If you change your behavior, you'll change your results.*

# NOW WHAT?

Something that was not possible in small town Zwolle, but was in Poznan, was clubbing. I went to clubs three to four times a week. They were packed with girls. There were so many of them, and I got very excited by this. Because Poznan was a student town, there was a fresh load of girls coming in every year from all over the world.

The beauty of women in Poland was also of a much higher standard than I was used to in the Netherlands. They were way more feminine and took better care of their appearance. They even dressed better. It was amazing, and I absolutely loved it from the start. My best friend in Poznan, remember Gucio? —DJ Andy Mile—was the DJ at all the main clubs. This gave me VIP access to all the parties, which in turn gave me access to more women.

I did my absolute best to leave behind my old behaviors and mindset and to fit in. These kids had no idea what my life had looked like back in my hometown, and they didn't have to know, either. I was really ready to let that all go because that wasn't really me anyway. In Poland, I would start a new life and learn to behave better and differently so I would get better, and different results.

People here did not use as many drugs as they did back home. This is not to say, however, that they didn't use them. Here it was more the occasional bump of cocaine in a club or a small joint on a Sunday evening. It wasn't like in Zwolle. They'd be stoned every minute of every day and sometimes wouldn't sleep for three days straight because of the speed they'd snorted.

I had experienced a few times that when I wore my jacket in a crowded club, a lot of people didn't see my arm was missing. I thought this was perfect. If people saw my arm was missing, I was scared

I would become 'the guy with one arm' to them, just like had happened in Zwolle. But many times in a crowed club, when I met new people, after we had already been talking for a few hours they suddenly asked 'Hey, what is wrong with your arm?' as if they just noticed it for the first time. I hated this question, but if they knew my personality already, they wouldn't judge me based on that. There were even people that told me, they didn't know I had one arm until someone told them later. These were people that I spent hours with in a club. They never noticed. My jacket was hiding my handicap, and became a safety blanket for me.

Luckily, going to prison was not a normal thing for the people I knew in Poznan. No one knew I had been to prison, and I kept it that way. I started running into problems I had not run into before. Good problems. How do I get these girls here? I had no experience with picking up girls in clubs, and no experience talking to women of such exceptional beauty.

I considered walking over to them and starting a conversation the entire time I was out. But I couldn't find the courage to do so. I'd stand in the corner and look at them, like some sort of creep. The longer I would stay there and think about approaching, the worse my anxiety got.

When I was introduced to girls, sometimes something would happen between us. But I felt I had little or no control over this. I basically took whatever I could get. I'd talk to a girl, hoping that I would be lucky enough to be selected by her. I'd have no idea if she liked me or not, and no idea how to have any influence on her feelings about me.

I would only hook up with women that I found to be averagely attractive. The women I found very attractive were interested in me at first, then I would get all excited and do my very best to start a relationship with them. Then they would lose interest.

I was too insecure to talk to the girls I really wanted, and at the same time too insecure to say no to girls I didn't want, because I didn't want to hurt their feelings, and I thought I couldn't get better anyway. If the next morning I figured out that I didn't even like this girl, I'd be very cold and distant and would not call her again. I'd even avoid her.

It got me the reputation that I was out to sleep with as many girls as I could. But that really wasn't true. I was really looking for a girl-friend, but I had no clue how. Those women of exceptional beauty that I saw in Poznan and really wanted? Forget about it. They were not available for men like me. Men that came from such a low social status and had such poor social skills. It wasn't in it for me.

In Zwolle, I could never have gained any experience in this area. Weekends in Zwolle were a joke! There were no clubs. There were bars, or—as I called them—stables packed with drunk farmers. Even if there was a bar that remotely resembled a club in Zwolle, the types of women there were in no way the calibre of women in Poznan — not even close.

# CHANGE YOUR BEHAVIOR

If I had a problem with my results, as I had figured out before, it meant there was a problem with my own behavior. Change your behavior, and you'll change your results.

I started reading books like -

*Superflirt*

*The Definitive Book of Body Language*

*Men Are from Mars, Women Are From Venus*

I read them over and over, anything I could get my hands on that would give me an idea of how to make the right impression on women and how to get them to sleep with me. My dream was to get a girlfriend who was pretty, from a normal environment, a normal family, who didn't hang out with junkies and criminals and who would know how to live a normal life that could help to make me feel good about myself.

I practiced my body language in front of the mirror and had a routine of how I would enter a club, how I would walk, and what my facial expression would be. Self-improvement was my main focus. My successes with women seemed to improve. It was definitely getting better.

I heard from Gucio that women were saying I was the most confident guy they'd ever met. This wasn't true at all, but the body language I had taught myself with the help of these books gave them that impression. My feelings were that I was still pretty insecure, though. I had no clue.

I always wore my leather jacket, even inside a club while I was sweating my ass off. When you saw me, you saw my leather jacket, my curtain, hiding my missing arm from the world. Always. No exceptions.

If someone did notice, I no longer resorted to violence if they asked what had happened. I'd still clench up, still want to strike, but I learned to control my urge. Really, I was just insecure.

For years I wore that jacket. When that jacket got so worn down and the color faded, I searched everywhere for a similar one. That jacket was my confidence.

Still, I did not seem to get the women I really wanted, but the ones I perceived as being just below that. This was already a step up for me. I constantly felt I was almost there.

After struggling like this for a few years, I started getting frustrated that I still did not find that dream girl I was looking for. Sure I slept around with women who I had a slight interest in, and it would give me a fleeting, mediocre satisfaction, but in the long run it made me feel terrible.

I felt I had no control over my love life.

# SCIENCE

One of the days I spent by myself in my apartment in Poznan, I saw something on a Dutch TV show. I always watched this show on a website which allowed me to watch Dutch TV shows while abroad. It was an anthropologist who had spent a few months undercover with a group of 'pickup artists' in the United States. He spoke to them, went out with them, slept at their houses, and became their friend.

He explained their tactics and what kind of theories they had based their findings on. The things he said made sense to me. They were very scientific. These guys tried out different tactics picking up girls on the street as well as in clubs. It was like scientific research in a laboratory. They wrote down their results, both good and bad, and had discovered a pattern in human dating habits that correlated very well with the Darwinian theories of evolutionary psychology.

I started Googling this *art* and came to understand that there was a worldwide community of pickup artists, the best of whom were dating coaches or instructors, who made their living traveling the world teaching people their skills. I found the whole science behind it fascinating, and the possibility of making money in this way, being a professional seducer, tickled my imagination.

One company, Love Systems, was the biggest and most famous with the best instructors working for them. After reading all their material and watching all their videos, I got a reasonable understanding of the theory and how it works in practice.

The main thing that resonated with me was to not be too eager. After reading their material I understood why I had no problem hooking up with women that I found a little attractive, but never hooked up with women that I found very attractive: I was too obvious.

There was no challenge, it made me boring to them. As for the less attractive girls, I was a challenge, because I wasn't sure. They'd still have to seduce me. This was just the start, there was so much more material, but at that time this was the most important chunk of information I could get out of it.

Beautiful women weren't more difficult to get, I just behaved differently. What was more difficult about a more beautiful woman had everything to do with how hard I found it to control my own behavior, and not with how beautiful she thought she was.

A girl I had my eye on for over a year, but didn't have much success with, ended up in my apartment the first night I went out with this knowledge. In the club I said a few lines to her that I learned from the Love Systems videos, and I did my best to not seem too eager, even though that was very hard, and it felt very uncomfortable.

All night, I fought not to stare at the diamond necklace she wore, dancing above her round breasts. I knew she wore it to tease my eyes, to lure them toward her cleavage. Her ass was well trained, round, and I looked at it each time she turned her back to me.

I told her about my cartoons, and she said she was very interested in seeing them. Awesome, an excuse to get her back to my place, I thought.

'Why don't you come with me and I'll show them to you, I live like two minutes away.'

'I would like that,' she answered.

*Holy fuck, this is going amazing,* I whispered to myself, desperately trying to figure out what to do next. I never thought I'd get this far. I ran out of all my material. We walked to my apartment. When we arrived I entered the apartment before her. She looked at me a bit surprised.

'You're a gentlemen I see.'

I had no idea what she meant by that.

'Hey, uh, you want a drink?' I asked her while taking her coat.

'Yes, thank you.'

'I only have vodka and coke.' I said and threw her jacket on one of my chairs. She stared at it.

'Ah, a real ladies drink. No, that's ok then, you have water?'

I did not have water. I never drank water. I drank coke, and if I wanted to get drunk, vodka and coke. That was all I had.

'Ehh... no, I'm sorry.'

'Don't be sorry, that's very unattractive.'

She sat down on the sofa as she spoke. This made me nervous. I sat down next to her, looking down at the floor.

'So uhhh... you uh... come to that club often?'

I instantly felt dumb as soon as the words came out of my mouth.

She looked at me with a questionable look.

'You know me, Mark, you see me there all the time. So, yes.'

She lit up a cigarette.

'Oh yes, you're right, I'm sorry.'

Apologizing again. This time she didn't bring me up on it, didn't even look in my direction.

'You have an ashtray?' She asked.

'Uh... I actually just use these empty cans of coke.'

I gave her a dented empty can that smelled like old cigarettes. She stared at it in disgust. She glanced around the room, at the mess on the floor, at the dirty glasses on the table half filled with three-day old cola. There was an old sock on the desk, surrounded by ashes from the joint Gucio and I smoked earlier that day. I'm sure it smelled like weed as well, a smell I was used to already. We went silent. She looked up at the spider webs on the ceiling and tapped her fingers repeatedly on the armrest of my sofa.

Tap. Tap. Tap. Tap.

I mustered up the courage to make my move. My heart rate was going up, I felt it throbbing in my chest and throat. I looked up to her, she looked at me and smiled with her lips pressed together and her eyebrows raised. She stopped tapping her fingers. I looked at her face for a few seconds.

*Should I kiss her? I dunno.*

'What are you doing?' She asked.

'Nothing.' I said. I looked down at the floor. A feeling of shame flooded through my body. My face turned red. I wanted to make my move, but didn't know how.

*Do I just go in for the kiss? Should I first make few jokes? Damn I dunno what to do!*

'You were going to show me your cartoons, right?'

I completely forgot.

'Oh yeah, you're right.'

I grabbed one of the magazines my comics were published in and gave it to her. I came in close with my face. I wanted to press my lips against hers.

'What are you doing?'

'Oh... I... uh...' I tried it again. She turned her head away and pushed me away with her hand against my chest. 'No, Mark, no.'

'Oh shit, I'm sorry, I'm so sorry...'

'That's ok, Mark. I'm going home anyway.'

'Yes, ok, uh... so, see you around, I guess.'

'Yeah, that's fine.'

She grabbed her coat and left.

I let myself fall backwards on the sofa. I grabbed my face with the palm of my hand, I squeezed my eyes shut. 'Oh my god... oh my god... oh my...' I mumbled over and over to myself.

I opened my eyes, and stared up to the ceiling. I smiled.

*That was... Amazing!*

A feeling of excitement came over me. That was the hottest girl I knew. The girl everyone I knew drooled over. She came back to my place. She was on my sofa. We were alone.

Something could have happened. It didn't, but it could have. It could have for sure. Before I would not even have been able to get this far. But this time, with a slight change in my behavior, I did. This was incredible.

'YES! YES!' I shouted, pounding my clenched fist against my chest. I poured myself a vodka and coke and stared at the wall. This was the best night of my life.

*If you'll change your behavior, you'll change your results.*

I knew if I wanted to learn more, I needed to be around the experts.

# DO IT WHILE SCARED

I had considered calling up Love Systems countless times, but was too nervous. It was a huge step for me. They were based in Los Angeles, and their phone number started with +1. For some reason, this was a big deal to me. I typed the number into Skype, but didn't press call the first time.

The second time I let it ring once but hung up. Finally, I let it ring. A guy named Jeremy picked up. Now there was no way back. I told him what I'd been doing in Poland, what improvements I had been making, but that I still wanted to learn some more. I told him I was considering becoming an instructor for Love Systems.

That was not so easy, he said. The Love Systems instructors were the best in the world and they trained for years before they even qualified for a consideration. Everyone wanted this job. They lived like rock stars, traveling the world, sleeping with beautiful women.

'But hey, go for it!' he said. 'It would be great to add you to the team if you ever reach that level!'

I knew I could do it. I had a feeling I'd be great at this.

It doesn't matter what it is. If you want to get good at something, you'll need to spend your time with people who are better at it than you. Otherwise, you won't learn, or at least not as fast. If your goal is to become a professional, you better spend your time with professionals, or you'll always be an amateur. Even if you have to get a job making them coffee, just be around them!

If you know you can do something, and really want to do it, get in touch with the people who are doing it. Do whatever it takes. You just need to get there, and you'll take it from there. If you're afraid, do it afraid.

I was considering it for a while. I wasn't sure. A weekend program cost $3,000, which was a lot of money. But if they would teach me what they said they would teach me, it would be worth it. I would also get in touch with the professionals, and who knew what would come from that.

'You're getting suckered into something,' someone said.

*Pussy.* People are always scared of change. They don't believe in things that don't fit into their reality, which is based on their experiences. The human mind has big problems accepting that other things are possible, things that don't align with what is already in their heads and within their map of reality. I had learned this already in my early days in Zwolle. If they have certain experiences, everything has to fit into those experiences, or it's just not possible, or at least so they think.

That's how the human mind works — mine as well as yours. Every once in awhile, you have to do something that will take you beyond your current experiences to broaden your horizon. That's how you grow. It was very similar to people in Zwolle saying, 'well, if Poland is that great, then why are all Poles coming over here?' Thinking based on their limited experience, not on facts.

This was way out of my comfort zone, but I wanted to do it. If you want change, you'll have to create it. If you'll keep doing what you've always done, you'll keep getting what you've always gotten. If you're scared, do it while scared, but do it above all else. This is the way to action change.

# JIM STARK

I took a boot camp, a three-day infield training, in Germany, right next to Poland.

We met in a tiny coffee shop, in Berlin, a three-hour train ride from Poznan. The place was filled with nervous looking men of all ages. They all had pads with them to write down notes during the seminar. Some of them were short and sat hunched over. Others were fat and wore glasses and blazers. One of them was biting his nails.

Four men swaggered in, brimming with confidence. They all had similar posture. They stood up straight, with their chins forward, but without trying. They were relaxed. *They must be the instructors*, I thought. A short, cheerful, Asian character stood tall in the middle. He introduced himself as Jim.

He wore a thin V-neck t-shirt, and worn down grey and blue sneakers with higher bottoms to make him seem taller. A permanent smile on his face showed all his teeth as well as a huge part of his gums. He spoke with an Australian accent, had sparkling brown eyes, and had a vibe around him that was contagious. Pure confidence, no overcompensation, he was himself and it was clear he was doing what he loved. Jim and I hit it off right away.

Whenever Jim liked something, he enthusiastically said 'Oh my god, that is sick!' 'Sick' was his word of choice. He stood in front of the room with his chest forward and began to speak.

'Hey guys, I will explain to you some very basic theory first. You can forget this, because it won't help you while talking to women, but I think it is useful to understand where the knowledge comes from, and on what principals we base our systems. Humans are evolutionarily designed to live in tribes. There was the tribal leader, who was the strongest and the protector of the tribe, and there were his friends. They were the only ones allowed to mate with women and create off-spring. The reason for this was, in those days' life was very danger-ous. Humans needed a strong tribe to survive, and women could only have children with men that could help her and her children survive, with men that would pass on the strongest genes.

If a woman would be stupid enough to have children with a man that was not the tribal leader, or at least aligned with the tribal lead-er, most likely she would die, and her kids as well. Women needed a man to survive, which is why even today women are attracted to a man's survival value, perceived through his behavior. Confidence is a great example of that and everyone knows women are attracted to confidence. This is because the only man in those days that would dare to be confident, was the tribal leader. No other man would be stupid enough to show any sign of cockiness or confidence, if he valued his life. Confidence by itself is not attractive, it is actually a very strong indicator that he possesses other attractive qualities. There are many more behavioral traits that women are attracted to, but confidence is a great example.

Men, on the other hand, needed women to replicate. They are attract-ed to her replication value. This is perceived through her looks. To this day, women are more attracted to a man's character and social status, and men are more attracted to a woman's appearance. This is why women spend so much money and time on make up, sexy dress-es, push up bras and hair. They know men are more attracted to them when they make themselves look pretty. It's all survival and repli-cation instincts. Or actually, it's only survival instincts. Replication means survival of the genes in the long term. This is also why the fear of rejection equals the fear of death for most men. This is not superfi-cial, it's the way we are evolutionarily designed. Deal with it.

But, the beauty of it is, in today's society, we can all become a trib-al leader. We can do the equivalent of what women do with their appearance, but with our behavior. Women make themselves more attractive by spending time on their looks. We can make ourselves more attractive by spending time on our behavior. We can all learn to be confident, we can all learn the traits a tribal leader would have in those days. The risk of getting killed is no longer there. There is nothing to fear. If we get great at portraying these behaviors, women can't help but be attracted to us. In the same way, men can't help but be attracted to beautiful women. Make no mistake, this is the basis for EVERY form of attraction between human beings. You can like it or not, you can be aware of it or not, it doesn't matter, this is the way it is, and has always been.

However, women's make up comes off at night, and their looks will fade as they get older. Our behavior will only develop over time. This is why lots of women say that older men are more attractive, if they know how to behave. This behavior will become a part of us. You will develop your character so that you will become a valuable man. In the beginning it will feel as if you're pretending, but that is true with everything you do for the first time. As you do it more often, it will feel natural, and you will become a naturally attractive man. It will take years of hard work and struggle, but eventually, you can just be yourself, your best self, and it will be perfect! Don't confuse attraction with love, though. Those are two different things. There is much more needed besides attraction to create a relationship. Attraction is merely step one, there is a long way to go from there. I will take you through all the steps, but let's focus on attraction for now, that is hard enough as it is.'

The way this guy spoke about picking up girls was on another level. His approach was scientific. He understood the workings of the brain, how the brain had developed, and how new habits are learned. He was so knowledgeable. He could speak for weeks on end about the subject without repeating himself. He had to edit his knowledge and tone it down a bit in order to fit it into a three-day program. He also put the information in chunks a regular person could understand. He did his best to avoid an 'information overload,' as he called it. Every second I spent talking to him, I learned something new. Jim continued talking, and I sat there with the others, enrapt.

'The reason why these women are so good at this, is because since they were 14 years old, every man has been trying to get with them. They can't help it. They are bored with it. They see right through all the phonies, because they have had so much practice. But, as soon as they meet a man that has the same experience, and approaches her in the right way, she will know it immediately. All her instincts and hormones will tell her in a split second that she should be attracted to him. Attraction is not a choice. If you do things right, you can have any woman you desire, believe me. A man will have to go out there and actively approach women, while a woman doesn't have to do anything. But with the right amount of effort, we are all able to gain the same experience. You need to approach and talk to as many women as you can, and improve yourself after each attempt.'

They taught me everything they could during the weekend, and we went out to the club to go hit on girls. The way these guys talked to women and the calibre of women they talked to blew my mind. They were the real deal.

I wore my leather jacket the entire time. Through the entire boot-camp, in the seminar, in the club, at lunch and dinner, my safety blanket was always there.

During the program Jim pointed at a girl and told me to talk to her. I was holding a drink at the time and told him I couldn't because I had no arm free. I hated not being able to move my arm while talking to girls. Since I only had one arm, that meant I couldn't approach any women while holding a drink.

Jim then proceeded to put both of his hands behind his back and approached the same girl. She definitely took a liking to him right away and was attracted. He walked back to me and said, 'so what was that about not having an arm free?'

I must have spoken to thirty girls a day during the program — one after the other with hardly any breaks. After each approach, one of the instructors told me what I could have done differently and how I could improve. It was intense, and I could see that not everyone was up for it. I loved it, however. It was incredible.

Approaching women you don't know is very scary. But, you have to do it anyway. When you're afraid, do it while being afraid. Good things will come from it.

'You have to understand, Mark. Our instincts tell us that we might die when we get rejected. It is literally the same fear as the fear of death. It's our instincts that tell us if a woman rejects us, the other women in the tribe will no longer want to mate with us, and we won't be able to pass on our genes; a fate worse than death. Or; maybe she is the woman of the tribal leader, and he will find out and kill you. But, this is not true in today's society.

This fear is irrational, and serves us no purpose. If one woman 'rejects' you, there is another one right behind her. The funny thing about it is, as soon as you start talking to the other woman, the woman who just rejected you might want you back. That's another instinct we still have. It happens literally every time we go out. It's like a toddler that isn't interested in a toy, until some other kid starts playing with it. You'll see, this becomes fun after a while.'

When the program ended, I spoke to Jim over dinner. I learned that his las name was Stark.

'Great, nice to meet you, Jim Stark.'

'Likewise, it's been a pleasure' he said with a squinting smile.

He told me he was also an online entrepreneur, making $2K a month with his online business selling shoes. This was amazing to me. If I could make $2K a month online, all my problems would be over. I'd be able to pay the bills, chill all day and smoke weed. That would be sweet. Somehow, success and entrepreneurs were just attracted to these guys.

If I could become one of them, these things would be attracted to me as well, I figured. This was exactly what I'd always dreamed about. In Zwolle, I was busy trying to become a big time weed dealer, which in retrospect was so stupid I have hardly any words for it. But If you gave me the choice between that or making money online, I'd choose the latter every time. I just never knew it was even an option.

I had chosen to change my life drastically once, and I was ready to do the same again.

I made it my goal to become a Love Systems instructor. I'd give anything to be one of them. If I possessed the skill set and the network these guys had, I could build a life being anything I wanted. Jim told me to email him the next day. He replied and offered me an internship. I would help out at programs, and in return I'd get to sit in on seminars and learn from them. He took a chance on me. I knew I was very rough around the edges. He wasn't sure. But I'd go to a seminar, do as I was told, and try to learn as much as I could.

I quit doing drugs entirely. No coke, no weed, nothing. Pure laser focus was all I wanted, nothing to cloud my mind. Even when I went out to the club, I didn't drink. My mind needed to be sharp at all times.

# BUILDING NEW SKILLS

Now the mission was to become the best dating coach on the planet. I needed to blow them away. Like with anything in life, practice makes perfect. I would devote every single minute of the day that I was awake to this.

If you want something, if you really want to do it, you'll do it. Not that you only want the result, but that you actually want to go through the process to get where you want to be. Then it will be a piece of cake. You have to want to put in the work to learn.

When you want to build a skill, but instead you lie on the couch and watch TV, apparently lying on the couch and watching TV is more important to you than building your skill. I'm not saying that is wrong. It's just what you want to do. It's a simple choice you make based on what you find most important and what you feel like doing. Make your choice. Your choice and your behavior will determine your results.

I read everything relevant I could find. I'd make notes during the boot camps I was assisting in and read through those. I internalized them. First thing in the morning, I was reading the theory, and the last thing at night, I was doing the same. I would approach at least five women a day, trying out different material, making notes, and improving.

On the weekends, I made twenty to thirty approaches a day, because there were more women around — both in the streets as well as in the club. My first approach outside boot camp was in Poznan in a famous shopping mall called Stary Browar, which means Old Brewery in Polish.

I saw a cute girl walking, shorter than me. She had shiny brown hair that was freshly dyed and pinned close to her head. Long curly tresses reached down to her shoulders and danced around while she walked on her high red stilettos. Yes, this was one of the women I found very attractive. Not just a little, but a lot.

My heart was pounding through my chest.

For some reason, I thought back to the heist Alvin and I pulled off back in Zwolle, where I walked past security like nothing was out of the ordinary.

*If you're frame of mind is strong, everyone will play along.*

I walked up to her and said in a loud voice, 'Hi!' while slightly touching the inside of her elbow with two fingers. My body language was confident, my back straight, and I made sure I kept strong eye contact, just like I'd learned from Jim.

She responded, 'Hi!'

I continued using pauses in my speech, building tension in our conversation.

'I saw you walking here... and just had to come over and talk to you... because I think... you... are... absolutely... adorable.'

She started smiling, and her eyes lit up. It was apparent she got excited by this. This had never happened to her before. We talked for a while and she gave me her phone number. That felt great. Not only did I conquer my own fear and got the result I wanted, I had clearly made her day as well. She was glowing.

This was something I had never considered possible before. Walk up to a girl and say that you like her, but don't make it seem as if you want her to be your girlfriend right away, or that you want to sleep with her. Just tell her you like the way she looks, and have a conversation. It's so simple, so obvious, yet no one seemed to do it. When I did do it, the girl enjoyed it so much. How could I have missed it?

Most people don't understand this is not about the girls. It's about you and overcoming your own fears. It's about constantly, deliberately putting yourself in stressful situations and controlling your own emotions. This builds character. You develop your social skills while gaining an incredible knowledge about yourself and managing emotions.

Your whole mind-set toward life changes. You start to recognize there are things that everyone you know considers to be impossible, but if you commit yourself and push yourself out of your comfort zone, those things are actually very possible. Soon the realization kicks in that there are tons of things out there you and everyone you know think can't be done, but they can. Your life is never the same after that.

The fear of rejection completely disappeared. The fear of rejection is, in fact, the fear of learning. Rejection is what makes you better. I learned way more from the approaches that did not go well than from the ones that did. Right away I'd know if it was my body language, my voice tonality, if I spoke too fast, or if my eye contact was off cue.

*There is no such thing as rejection, only feedback.*

I made a deal with myself that I would get rejected five times a day, no matter what. Even when I was sick, I'd go outside and approach five women and hope to get rejected by them quickly, so I could go home.

Me: 'Hi!'
Her: 'Fuck off, creep!'

Me: 'So... can I have your number?'
Her: 'No way. I don't even know you. You might be a rapist. Ewww get away from me!'

Me: 'Hey you are really cute. Where are you from?'
Her: Giving me a look like I'm disgusting and walking away.

Me: 'You're very sexy!'
Her: 'Ooookaaaaaayyyyy. Ehhhhh... I'm going over there... bye!'

Those are only a few examples of the thousands of rejections I've had. That is not an exaggeration, literally thousands of rejections piled on top of each other. It gave me razor-sharp feeling for what did not work, and I started to understand very well what did work.

*An expert is a man who has made all the mistakes that can be made, in a narrow field.*

# MARK V

What I quickly learned was that telling women how popular, cool, or successful you are, doesn't work. Only the extremely stupid women will fall for that — women who have never been around popular, successful men and don't understand how these men would behave.

A beautiful woman, who has had many successful male suitors in her life, picks all of this up by his non-verbal sub-communications. It's not what he says, but how he says it. She has seen so many men try and impress her in any way possible, that from personal experience alone she knows what is bullshit and what is not.

Whenever I told a woman, or even hinted, I'm rich or successful, I usually just got a dirty look, or she'd laugh at me. It wouldn't matter if it's true or not. Even when I told a woman that my comics were nationally published in the Netherlands, which was true, it would get me a questionable look from her. If this would become clear in a natural way, then it would be great. But if I'd have to tell her, and it seemed to her that I was trying to impress her with this, it would get me the opposite result. Just the fact that I was trying to impress her would be unimpressive. Even if the thing I'm trying to impress her with is impressive in and by itself.

These women are so experienced at this, they really see right through you. It's why a lot of men think that 'all hot girls are bitches' or 'all beautiful women think they are better than everyone else.' This is not true, you see. They only pick up on your bullshit way quicker, and don't waste their time talking to someone that is coming off as fake.

What does work though, is to make sure you have strong and confident body language. Make sure that you are a socially savvy person, and don't try to make yourself seem better than you are. Your manners will sub-communicate to her what kind of man you are, and it will be way more effective to non-verbally communicate your attractive qualities.

Keep the frame of mind that you are a regular guy talking to a regular girl. If your frame of mind is strong, everyone will play along.

With every boot camp I assisted, I got better and better. I'd demo approaches on girls live in the club while students were watching. I'd talk to girls with students, helping them attract the women they wanted, while keeping their friends entertained. People started talking about me, and a legend around Mark V (which was now my nickname) was created. Apparently they all thought that I could get every woman, every time I wanted.

This obviously wasn't true. I constantly told them this. During the bootcamps the perfect conditions were created for me to talk to and seduce certain women, and that's what I demonstrated. These were not necessarily the women I'd choose in my real life.

When I was asked how come I had no fear of walking up to women in clubs and starting a conversation, I'd explain that a club is just a room with flashy lights, that's it. It's a room, just like any room in my own house. It's a room filled with people, people like me. These women are mainly little girls that are just discovering the world like the rest of us. They are more confused than I am, and they have no clue either. They are younger and know less about life than me. In no way am I impressed or intimidated by any of this.

Students posted reviews on the forums about the boot camps I assisted -

'I have to give a special thanks to Mark V. He worked with me mostly in field. Mark, you're amazing, man! I'll never forget how you made me approach those two girls by walking all the way across the room like I owned the place. Thanks man, I'll never forget it!' ~ Steven R.

'Mark V, this guy mastered body language. I have seen him sit silently next to a girl for fifteen minutes before making out with her. It was amazing!' ~ John D.

'Mark V showed me that you have to stand tall and speak up. I seriously love that guy!' ~ Derek W

'I could see how both Jim and Mark V would speak to girls that I was talking to before without much success, and the girls would just... well... melt. It was incredible to just watch that scene unfold in front of me.' ~ William H

'Mark V explained to me, 'The thing about attraction, Damian, is that it's measured by the amount of compliance you're getting. Make her a suggestion like, 'Hey let's go over there,' and see if she follows. If she does, you can assume attraction. Getting her to high five you, and her letting you fuck her up the ass, is both compliance. It's just that one is a small level of compliance, and requires a little attraction, the other is a high level of compliance and requires a lot of attraction. This can be escalated. You start low and end high, but it's basically the same thing.'

I'm still laughing as I write this.' ~ Damian H

I loved reading those reviews. My efforts were really getting noticed, and it showed people what was possible. I compared it to being a football player. If you want to play football, practicing it every day will make you a better player.

If you're a professional football player, you will not make every shot, you'll not make every goal, not every pass will be perfect, and you won't win every game. But when you do, it's legendary, and you're a hero. You're able to improve your technique with years of discipline, dedication and practice, and every once in awhile, you'll make a shot or goal that no amateur can make.

I still wore my black leather jacket everywhere.

When people asked me why, I'd tell them that I just liked my jacket, what about it? People were very impressed that I was not bothered by having one arm, and I told everyone that I wasn't. But me wearing my jacket in the club was a safety blanket I used because I subconsciously thought women would judge me for it if that was their first impression of me. I'd been doing this for a very long time.

Jim told me that he had received complaints about me from other instructors. They found me to be a show off, and that I bragged too much about my successes with women. I also made inappropriate jokes at the wrong times. They found this annoying and disruptive. It was really jeopardizing my chances of making it to be a pro.

At first I was offended by this. Where do they come off? Also, why couldn't they tell me this to my face? I got angry. I didn't understand. I thought everyone liked me and I was doing a great job.

*Fuck those guys.*

# PROJECT ROCK STAR

Jim started a program called Project Rock Star.

Project Rock Star was an intensive, twelve-week course where a few lucky people were selected to get training from the best instructors for free. The participants were selected based on the value they'd bring to the instructors' lives. These were mainly entrepreneurs, but also people with contacts in politics and other things that might come in handy.

In 2010, the program was led by an instructor who went by the name of Jeremy Soul. He was the author of the book Daytime Dating. He was the world's foremost expert in meeting women during the day in the street. I was very impressed by him. He was also a very funny guy and great to be around. Soul was of Sri Lankan descent. He had brown skin. He wore glasses. His laugh was loud and ostentatious, drawing attention whenever he found something funny.

He asked me to be an instructor for Project Rock Star. Fuck yeah.

Jim told me that Project Rock Star would be a make or break opportunity for me. If I managed to impress the other instructors, they would put in a good word for me with Nick, the CEO, and I could be in. If, on the other hand, I did not improve, it would be catastrophic.

Now was the time I had to impress the other instructors. Not only in skill, but also in my behavior.

*Pressure. Just what I needed. Perfect.*

The following week I was in Poznan and opened my email inbox on my laptop. There was an email in there from one of the company's top instructors, who went by the nickname Chris Shepherd. He was one of the original guys back from when the company was still called The Mystery Method, after the founder of the company, the illusionist, 'Mystery'.

He and Cajun, another top instructor, were holding a bootcamp in Toronto, and they needed an extra instructor to manage three more students. No one else had time to do it. That's why they had sent out an email to the list of prospective instructors, which I was now a part of.

Cajun gained worldwide fame after he went on the TV show *Keys to the VIP*, where guys competed against each other to pick up girls with cameras rolling. The judges of the show were blown away by him and said they had never seen anything like it. All his approaches were on the most beautiful girls in the club, and they all went perfectly.

I replied that I had the time to do it, and that I was dying to go. Chris was skeptical at first, he didn't know me, but other instructors vouched for me so he agreed. Jim was the one who pushed me forward. I was sure of that. An hour later, I had a ticket to Toronto in my inbox, all expenses paid. I would leave in two days.

This would actually be at the same time Project Rock Star would start, which meant I would miss the first week of the twelve-week program. It didn't matter because it gave me the opportunity to work with two of the world's most skilled dating coaches. Chris and Cajun were absolute legends. Their videos were all over YouTube. There was no way I would skip on that opportunity.

Chris and Cajun were great, an absolute pleasure to be around. They were both shorter than me, but Cajun, especially, was tiny. They both had brown hair and spoke with a Canadian accent, saying 'eh' all the time.

'So let's go ever here, eh?'

'We're having pancakes for breakfast, eh?'

We did the boot camp and went camping in the woods in Canada afterwards. These guys were funny and quite crazy. I remember we were playing poker and Cajun kept winning. Then Chris said he was not allowed to deal the cards any longer. Cajun started losing. After he lost all his chips, we allowed him to rejoin the game, if all of us got to shoot him in the ass once with a BB gun. That was Chris' idea.

We got completely shitfaced on whiskey and sprite. In the morning we had pancakes with Canadian maple syrup for breakfast. It was legendary.

# CHARLES NGO

From Toronto, I flew straight to London, where Project Rock Star had already started. From the airport I went to Jim's house where I spent the night. In the morning he told me to go to the seminar, where all the students would be waiting.

At the seminar, I met the rest of the guys for the first time. There was an international car dealer from Morocco who grew up in France, named Laurent. He was tall and had long, curly brown hair, which he tied in a pony tail. His trousers were hanging halfway down his ass, but he wore it with style.

One of the guys was the chewing gum king of Chicago, owning a huge portfolio of gum ball machines in shopping malls across the city.

Another one of the group was a professional skydiver.

There were two brothers from Dubai, Adnan and Joseph Procer, who were life coaches and practiced NLP. They knew a lot about people and what made them tick. They were able to hypnotize people in order to teach them new habits, or get rid of old ones, they told me.

They were both slim, in great shape, tall and had brown hair and big noses. They spoke with an Arabic accent, which I thought sounded funny. These guys gave me the same feeling Kasper from back in Zwolle used to give me. I just had to be honest with them. Pretending to them would be futile, they'd see right through me. They were warm, kind-hearted souls.

These were the types of people who were there. But one of them would impact my life more than the others countless times — Charles

Ngo. Charles was not a student of the program. He only flew in to teach a seminar. He was friends with a couple of guys in the program and was invited over to help out. He was such a great guy that he did it with pleasure.

Charles was an Internet marketer. He had made millions selling diet pills and skin care products online. It was already my dream to make $2K a month online, like Jim was doing at the time, but this guy was on a whole other level. Charles was a short Asian guy, cute-looking in a childlike way. He stood up straight, had great posture, and spoke with a soft voice. Charles wore a suit and tie. He was introverted and the only times he got social was when speaking about marketing, or video games.

He gave us a three-day seminar on the way his industry worked and how to get started. He showed us the advertisements he'd made in the past, and for which products they were created. He showed us affiliate networks and traffic sources like Facebook and Google, where anyone could create an advertising account and start advertising.

He told us how there was a twenty-one-year-old guy from Canada who sold half a billion dollars' worth of diet pills, teeth whitening gel, and skin care products by using affiliate marketing. He showed us that on the Internet, if you're creative, work hard, and are smart enough to control your damage when things don't go your way, you could get rich.

'All an affiliate marketer does, is come up with marketing angles, test out the new angles online, and collect data. It's all trial and error. You look for patterns in peoples behavior. You look at click through ratios, conversion ratios, you divide them up in age groups, cities, gender, education level, and look for patterns. Until you find that sweet spot. The right ad, with the right target audience, for the right product, on the right website.'

When I heard this, something clicked. It just hit me. All I've been doing this whole time was collect data, and look for patterns in human behavior. I've done this with dating. It's all been trial and error until I found a pattern that worked, and I applied it to every woman I met. The club in which I met my women was comparable with the website Charles displayed his ads on. It's a place with lots of traffic, a place lots of people visit. The opening line I used were my marketing angles, they were my ads. The women I approached were my impressions. The percentage of women that engaged in a conversion with me was my click through ratio. The percentage women that slept with me was my conversion ratio. What I've been doing to my dating life, I can apply to online marketing.

It was so obvious to me, I sat there and listened to Charles, while he continued.

His eyes sparkled when he spoke about some tricks he pulled off to get cheaper traffic to his websites. He showed us a head line 'Are You a Muffin Top?' with a picture of a woman that had her belly fat stick out of her trousers while riding a bike. This ad was targeted at females 30+ on Facebook.

'Haha! oh man that is so great! People really click on those ads and buy products?'

'Yeah man, how do you think Facebook makes money? They sell advertisements, and guys like me use them to sell products for other companies,' Charles explained.

'Shit, I can't believe it. I would never click on an ad like that, and I would never buy a product like that online from some random website.'

'Yeah well, you are a bit smarter than most people, Mark. Most people aren't really that clever. To be honest, I shouldn't say this, but most people are kinda dumb.'

It reminded me of all the dumb people I grew up around in Zwolle. I fought off the anger these memories created in me. In a slightly annoyed tone I said, 'Yeah, I fucking HATE all those dumb people man. Fuck them.'

Charles looked at me surprised. *Oh shit, I said something wrong,* I thought.

'No, you gotta love those people, man. Those are the ones buying your products. Don't shoot yourself in the foot by hating those people. They are the ones that will make you rich!'

*Good point.*

# GROWN UP TALK

We went out with the students every day, talking with them to women on the street during the day and in a club at night. In between, we held seminars.

Jim gave some harsh criticism to Laurent. I could tell he was taking it very hard. Jim can be brutally honest. That's what I liked about him. But sometimes he went a bit too far. When we all went out for lunch, Laurent was walking at the back of the group. Hunched over, looking at the ground with a sad face. I told Laurent not to worry, I liked him from the start and didn't necessarily agree with Jim.

'To be honest, the first time I met you I thought that you were a really cool guy.'

He cheered up immediately, put his arm around me, smiled big while looking up at the sky, and picked up the pace in his walk. I was working extremely hard to teach the students as much as I could. My impression was that it went great. One day I got a call from Jim, though.

'Mark, listen. Soul called me. Have you been bragging to him about girls you've picked up?'

I remembered a conversation I had with Soul over dinner. He was telling me about girls that he'd slept with, and in return I told him about some of mine. It's what guys do, right? Just shooting the shit, talking about girls. I didn't really see what I did wrong.

'No I haven't, we were just talking! Did he say that?'

'What you need to understand, Mark, is that these people aren't interested in that. Why would you tell them that? They don't care.'

'But he started it.'

'Listen, man, that doesn't matter. Keep in mind this one rule. Never talk to instructors about your girls under any circumstances. When they speak to you about it, let them, but don't join in.'

It shattered my mood. My feeling was that I was doing a great job. I was putting in my time and effort. I spoke once about it with an instructor after he started the topic, and right away I got punished like this. It felt really unfair. From that day on, I was no longer happy at Project Rock Star.

The next day I sent a text to Jim saying I was sorry, but I didn't know what I could do to make the other instructors happy. I'd just go back to Poland.

'Thanks for everything, but I'm leaving.'

He texted me back and told me to come to his apartment right away. I did. We had a very long talk about why I behaved like that and why it's a problem to more experienced instructors.

'Look, man. Everyone here is good at picking up girls, everyone. You, me, all the others, they all know what they are doing. Everyone has their own style and personality, but in general, everyone here knows their shit. You will not ever impress any of these guys with how good you are at this. The only thing it will do is make them wonder why you are trying so hard.'

His insights on social dynamics were of a level I'd never experienced. He took three hours out of his day to explain to me why it's annoying to people who are experts at something to hear a beginner tell them how good they are.

'You might think you are hot shit, Mark. But you're not. You might be in the future, but not now. But, by the time you will be on the same expert level as these other instructors, you won't feel the need any longer to constantly prove yourself, and your voice tonality and sub-communication will change when you do speak about it.'

As the conversation progressed, I indeed realized that the best guys never spoke about their successes. All the best guys just did what they did without ever mentioning it. It was business as usual.

'Yes, compared to all the people you've ever met before, you might know more than anyone, and they might be very interested to hear you speak. But these guys are the best in the world, Mark. You are nobody. It's in your best interest to not say anything and be cool to everyone.'

I remembered that when I spoke to women, I never bragged about anything. These women hear guys brag all the time. They are allergic to it. What really impresses them is just being yourself and not trying to be better than that. That's true confidence.

With women, I knew this. It was one of the reasons it was doing so well. So why did I think guys were any different?

If I avoided bragging to women because I knew they would be turned off by this, why was I trying to impress the other instructors by bragging to them? Women aren't the only ones turned off by that. Everyone was.

People hate bragging, even if you don't mean it like that. People hate it when you're constantly seeking the approval of others, especially people of value. You'd impress people more by acting like a normal person and showing an interest. I told Jim I would change. I understood it then.

# PEOPLE LIKE YOU BY DEFAULT

In the morning I spoke to Joseph, the oldest of the two brothers from Dubai. I asked him how the hypnosis that he and his brother practiced worked. After hearing his explanation, I told him I still had some baggage left from my past life, and I believed it was making me come off as a douchebag at times.

'Yes, I know that about you. I can see your life has been hard. But I can also see that you are a good person, and you mean well,' he told me.

'Do you think hypnosis might help me?' I was willing to try anything.

'We can try doing an NLP session, if you're up for it. We'll see how you respond.'

Being hypnotized is quite a pleasant experience. It's not like in the movies where they swing a watch in front of your eyes and say things like, 'you're getting very sleeeepyyyyy...' No, not at all. I laid down on the sofa, and Joseph spoke to me in a calm voice. I was still awake, but in a different state of mind. I was very relaxed and open. While in this state, Joseph asked me why I was behaving the way I was.

'I just feel I always have to make everyone laugh, and impress everyone with my knowledge and skills, in order to get their respect and appreciation.'

'Why?'

'I dunno, I mean... I guess I feel that if I wouldn't get attention, no one would even notice me and no one would like me.' I said with my eyes closed.

'Have you always been like that? Because that is not true at all. What was your childhood like?'

I told him the whole story. It became clear this was behavior I had picked up in my youth. Being picked on in school and the constant disapproval of authority figures created a deeply rooted urge to prove my worthiness to others.

In my childhood, I would get all violent and aggressive. That was my way of controlling my environment. Back then I needed everyone to know that I was the kind of person that would resort to violence if needed. Now that I was no longer a violent person, I still felt I needed to constantly let everyone know who I was, and why they should respect me. It was the same insecurity, and the same defense mechanism. It only took a different form.

I had successfully left behind my criminal and aggressive behavior, but that wasn't enough yet to live up to the social standards of the group of people I wanted to belong to. I needed to erase the emotional scars left in my character.

'Mark, people like you by default, remember that. If you do nothing, everyone will always like you. Trying to make people like you can only make them like you less. Everyone always assumes you're a good person, unless you give them a reason not to.'

He spoke in a calm and slow voice, with a certain pace that made it stick in my head.

'If you give them the feeling you have to prove to them you are a good person, they will assume you're not a good person. Why else would you have to prove it?'

He was very wise. While hearing him talk, I had the exact same reaction and realization as I did in my previous conversation with Jim, which was that when I talked to women, I knew this already.

Jim had already made me come to the same conclusion before, without me being under hypnosis. But Joseph dropped another truth bomb then that made me let go of my past, even more than I had already done.

'People like you by default. Everyone likes you.'

He repeated this again in a calm and slow voice. It really stuck in my head. This realization is one of the most important triggers of change in my life, after being robbed.

*People like you by default. Everyone likes you, unless you give them a reason not to.*

The next day I was teaching a day-game workshop with Soul. We gave a seminar and then took students out into the street to help them speak to girls. During the whole program, I kept my mouth shut. If someone asked me a question, I would give a short, clear answer and go back to being silent. My whole focus was on letting Soul lead the program, and not be in his way.

I was his assistant and only played that role. During the program I got the chance to speak to Soul, and I just asked it to him straight. I wanted to know what the problem was. Soul told me that he didn't get the feeling that I was showing any interest in other people. I was so busy with my own progress and showing everyone how cool I thought I was that I never took the time to really get to know him or anyone else.

As an example, he asked me if I even knew his father was very ill in the hospital, and that he was constantly worried about it. I knew this, but I didn't want to bother him by bringing it up.

'That's stupid,' he said. 'People appreciate it when you take an interest. Have you ever asked me anything personal, like if I have brothers or sisters?'

I had not.

'Do you have any brothers or sisters?' I asked him.

He smiled and told me that he had. Now we started talking. I actually incorporated that line into my standard routine while talking
to women.

'Do you have any brothers or sisters?' It builds rapport. I taught this
to students. They loved it.

During the conversation Soul asked me what I had said to the girl
earlier in the program when I was doing a demonstration. How I
managed to get her number. My first instinct was to tell him in de-
tail what I had done and how I did it. But I remembered my talk
with Jim. I told Soul I didn't feel like telling him. It was nothing
special, I said.

'Ah come on, man, I really want to know!'

'No, it's ok. Let's talk about something else. So how is your dad
doing?'

That evening I got a call from Jim. 'Mark, I don't know what you've
done. But Soul just called me. He is extremely impressed.'

That's where I grasped to the full extent that being modest is way
more impressive than telling people how good you are. If you're
good at something, other people who are good at this will recognize
it anyway. Soul did, without me telling him. Game recognizes game.
Trying to tell people how good you are will get you the opposite

result. It's low-value behavior. Only people who are overcompensating do that.

Experts don't need to prove they are experts. They are not in search of validation from anyone. This is something that really bothers me in people now, and it's actually a very common behavioral trait. I hate the way I used to behave. Just assume everyone likes you by default unless you give them a reason not to.

If you're not good at something, and just keep quiet, you might learn something. Because now the more experienced people will have a chance to talk, and you have a chance to listen. If you're not that good at something, but are trying to act like you are, the people who are good at it will think you're an idiot and will not want to have anything to do with you, thus cutting you off from a valuable source of information.

Talking about yourself, telling people how good you are, will only impress the inexperienced people. This will surround you with people that can't teach you anything, and you'll spiral down again. You need good people around you, and the only way to get and keep them around you is by knowing how to behave. Being modest attracts the right people, while coming off as bragging attracts the wrong people and pushes the right people away.

Act normal. It's nothing special, and you're nothing special. It's way more important to give people good emotions by showing them respect. Good emotions are valuable, and if you give people good emotions, they'll perceive you as valuable.

# GAME CHANGER

We were out in the club with all the students. Jim asked me for the first time, 'Why are you wearing your jacket?'

For the first time I decided to be honest.

'Have you tried it without a jacket?' he asked me. 'Because I don't think it would make any difference. It's just something you're telling yourself, but it's probably all in your head. To be honest, Mark, everyone sees you have one arm, with or without a jacket.'

I stood there thinking.

*He was right.*

Straight away I went to the coat closet of the club and gave them my jacket to hang. I went back into the club to start demonstrating approaches on women for students. Every demonstration I did went amazing after that. You can imagine my surprise. It's not just that these women were not bothered that I have one arm. They seemed to like me more, because of it. All this time I was telling myself it was holding me back. But actually, the belief that it was holding me back was holding me back. I might have also looked weird wearing my jacket, I realized. The next week, Jim and I went to the beach. I approached a few girls without a shirt on, openly showing the scars on my arm. It made literally no difference. The girls became attracted, just like they normally would.

I was worried about nothing, all this time. I wrote a short article about it. This article was shared throughout the community worldwide and made me famous in the industry.

# WHY HAVING A DISABILITY HELPS MY GAME

And how YOU can have the life you want, no matter what hand you were dealt.

By Mark V, prospective Love Systems instructor

As some of you might know, I was hit by a tram when I was five years old and lost my entire right arm from the shoulder down. I'm not going to tell you the whole sob story about growing up like that. All you need to know is that it sucked and I felt like shit. It made me insecure. That's in the past now, but there was always this doubt that I would be able to hook up with hot, popular girls. Nothing would be further from the truth...

I have examined this thing in different ways from a few angles. And having one arm, missing a leg, having a limp, crooked eyes, or just being overweight is actually... well, something that sets you apart. In a good way. What Savoy called a 'Demonstration of Higher Value' in the Magic Bullets Handbook, a DHV.

I don't care what you have. If you are completely comfortable with it, and if you show it in everything that you do, it becomes an attractive quality. If on top of that you're good at Love Systems, you have an advantage over what others wish they could have.

A few advantages I have come across are:

> It shows vulnerability. That doesn't get you very far by itself, but if you also have the Love Systems skills of being able to convey dominance and sexualization, it's incredibly powerful.
> It can create an instant connection and rapport. Everyone's got something. For example, a dancer I recently

picked up immediately showed me a scar she had from when she was a kid.

> It makes you more interesting because you must have overcome a lot to be where you are.
> You're just different, period.
> It completely short-circuits the 'player' vibe.

There are many more, but you get the point.

Let's get specific. I'll use common questions I get from women about my arm as examples; you should have no trouble applying this to whatever it is you think is holding you back.

'Is there something wrong with your arm?'

In the past, if a girl asked me this, I would get all tense and in my head I'd be thinking, 'I hope she doesn't mind.' Now if a girl asks me that, I respond enthusiastically, 'that's right, baby, one arm!' Women love it, and it shows that you hold your own, no matter what.

'What happened to your arm?'

If you're anything like me, you get annoyed by this kind of question, especially the 500th time you're asked. But if you show annoyance or give a ridiculous answer, you are only sub-communicating that you are uncomfortable with it. That's never good. Instead, just answer the question. 'Oh, I had an accident when I was a kid.' Then change the subject — like you do with Love Systems any time there's a conversation topic that isn't going to help you, whether it's about your missing arm, her boyfriend, or why she has to get up early tomorrow. 'Have you met my friend Andrew?'

Because only someone with a strong personality and a lot going for him would cope with such a big problem so well, it becomes a DHV.

More questions about the arm...

Don't start answering a string of questions about it and get stuck in a long conversation about your 'handicap.' You don't want to be 'the handicapped guy.' I'm sure you've listened to the interview with Future, Sinn, and Tenmagnet on Identity, so you know how women will apply an identity to you based on your first conversation. (If not, get it now. To get good, you need to spend time APPLYING knowledge to your own game. There isn't time in any man's life to reinvent the wheel. Learn the shortcuts from people who came before you. I definitely have.)

If she really wants to know more about the arm, she's going to have to work for it. Why would you open up that much to someone you just met? After you've closed the deal and are lying naked in bed, then you can tell her anything you want. It will only make her love you more.

In summary, when a woman asks you about the thing that makes you different... don't be insecure, and don't be defensive. Think: GAME ON!

~ Mark V

And that, beyond my previous creative work of course, was my introduction to being a recognized writer in the field. That article was about my physical disability, and how I overcame it.

But anxiety is a disability. Every man experiences anxiety before approaching a woman, it's only natural. It's our evolved instincts telling us there is danger in rejection. It's an irrational fear left over from our hunter gatherer days. You need to approach anxiety the way I've approached my only having one arm, as something that you need to forget. Approach anxiety with that same confidence, that self assuredness and it'll fall under your grasp. Don't think, just fucking do it, and it will all work out. If you're scared, do it while scared, but fucking do it anyway.

*Look at her. You see her standing there. She lures your eyes in every few seconds. She makes you nervous. You would love to speak to her, but you can't. No way she'd be into you. Who are you? Why would she want you? You better just stay in your own world, don't get any funny ideas.*

*Your heart rate goes up, your palms get sweaty. The longer you wait the worse it gets.*

*Maybe if you could get introduced to her, then maybe you might try and make your move. But besides that, why would she want to talk to you? There is no way in hell. All of that is in your own head. Who says she does not want to talk to you? Why wouldn't she? She is most likely looking for a man, and you are one. The reason she wears that dress, the reason she spent an hour putting on that make up, is because she wants to meet you.*

*Everything you can come up with preventing you from speaking to her is some bullshit story you tell yourself.*

# SAYING GOODBYE

On the final day of Rock Star, Soul got us five tables at an exclusive club in Stockholm, Sweden. He invited everyone he knew. We were there with at least sixty guys. All these guys were highly trained in dating science and successful entrepreneurs. We created and controlled the whole vibe of the club.

Those tables were filled with bottles of champagne, vodka, whiskey and all sorts of soft drinks. Two blonde girls that caught the eye of the whole place were in the middle of the room. Every guy was paying attention to them. These were your typical Swedish blonde bombshells.

I entered the club. I was a bit late because I did a boot camp in a different club, and I was still wearing my jacket. This time not as a safety blanket but pure coincidence. Out of habit, I started approaching every girl I saw. I got shut down three times in a row until I walked up to the two girls who were the center of attention and started speaking to the one I perceived as being the most beautiful.

'Hi! My name is mark.' I told her in her ear, then leaned back and created eye contact. 'I just had to come over here and meet you.'

'Oh hi' she replied and introduced herself.

Her eyes were bright blue. She wore a long white dress that night, under it grey sparkly shoes. Her teeth were the same color as her dress. She smiled broadly, dimpling her cheeks.

'I do know that your are absolutely gorgeous, but what else is interesting about you besides your looks? I don't talk to just anybody, you know...'

She gave me a look that told me as much as 'Who do you think you are?'

'Where are you from?' I continued.

We spoke for about an hour when I started noticing something strange. She was showing all the signs I always teach students to look for — the signs that tell you she is clearly attracted to you. But regular girls would already be willing to kiss at this stage, and she was not. This confused me.

There was a trick I always used in these situations. A situation where you don't know where this is going. Say something shocking and bold, something that makes it 100-percent clear to her that you want to take this interaction further in a sexual way. If after that, she is still talking to you, you know she has accepted your intentions and it will most likely go in the direction you want.

If she gets offended and walks away, it probably wasn't going any-where anyway, and you won't waste any more of your time. I moved in close to her, and said, using pauses in my speech,

'I think you're a great girl... and I'm really enjoying this conversa-tion... but... if we're not going to be making out soon... I'm gonna have to start talking... to some other girls.'

Her eyes lit up and she smiled. She could not believe what I just said to her. No slap in my face, and she was still sitting there, giving me the same signs. This was looking good, but still no kiss. Weird.

'Come with me,' I said, grabbing her hand, and walked to the bar.

I started introducing her to random people I knew to build social proof. All these guys were trained by us, so they knew exactly how to respond. The dumbest thing guys usually do is try to take each other's women. We teach guys to work together. Don't compete, but help each other.

'Hey, meet my friend, Jerry!'

Jerry replies with, 'How do you know Mark? Let me tell you this guy is AMAZING. He is awesome!'

'Meet my buddy, Shane.'

'Oh my god, how do you know Mark? Mark is awesome!'

After the third guy I introduced her to, she had a big smile on her face and said, 'Everyone keeps saying that!'

This could not have gone any better, but still no kissing. I had never experienced this. The club was closing so we left. I grabbed her hand and said 'we're going to my hotel.' Around the corner we started kissing, finally. In the hotel room my jacket came off. She had actually not noticed yet that I had one arm. She was too busy looking into my eyes, I guess.

'Oh my god, you have one arm. That is SO COOL!'

The next day I Googled her name. There were tons of hits. I looked at Google images and saw pages and pages of her pictures all over the Internet, in magazines, tabloids, you name it. Turned out, she was a local celebrity, and I did not even know it. This explained why she wouldn't kiss me in the club. She did not want any pictures showing up on websites or in magazines. Makes sense. I don't think I would have wanted that either.

If I had known she was a celebrity, this would have probably screwed with my emotions, and I would have blown it. However, I didn't know, so I behaved to her like I did with every other woman, and she responded like every other woman would. Everything is in your own head. That she was famous made no difference, as long as I did not behave differently myself.

This adds up to what I was saying before. All your results depend on your own behavior. Change your behavior, and you'll change your results.

I tried to call her the next day, but got no answer. She did not reply to my texts either. I got really annoyed by it and sent her a final text saying that she might think I was only after sex, but she was wrong.

A few days later, I got a very long private message from her on Facebook. Turns out, I wasn't the only one who had done some name Googling. She found out who I was too. She found pages and pages of ex-students telling highly exaggerated stories of how many girls I'd slept with. There was even a blog post from a student who described how I picked her up, a blog post about exactly that night when I met her, and how I got her back to my hotel.

She was not amused, to say the least. I told her that in my opinion she was acting very childish, and we exchanged a few words I do not care to repeat. She wanted to 'stay friends' but I didn't want to. Later, I thought this might have been code for 'Let's hook up again later,' although it might not have been. I will never know.

I never spoke to her again.

# RYAN BUKE

Project Rockstar was over, and I went back to Poznan. After speaking to Charles about Internet marketing, I made it my new mission to make it in that business. After this journey, I had learned that anything can be achieved if you dedicated yourself to it relentlessly. If you applied laser focus and learned from the right people, you could do whatever you wanted.

I sat behind my desk and Googled 'affiliate marketing.' There were tons of blogs and websites about the subject. On these blogs I saw 19-year-old kids driving Ferraris. I read stories about kids making $20k a day living in their parents' basements.

These kids travelled the world first class. They had car parks filled with Bentleys, Lamborghini's, and Rolls Royces. They slept in the most expensive hotels. I found it fascinating, incredible and exciting.

I tried to apply for accounts with a few affiliate networks but was denied. I bought a wedding website on flippa.com for $100. I figured I could sell wedding related products on it. It didn't go well. I tried buying and selling things on eBay. It went even worse. Soon, I felt I had no idea where to even start. I wished I had someone to learn from. I needed a Jim Stark of affiliate marketing — someone who could teach me everything he knew. In the interim I started reading books like:

*The 7 Habits of Highly Effective People*

*The 4-Hour Work Week*

*Secrets of the Millionaire Mind*

*Ca$hvertising*

*Lifestyle Entrepreneur*

I still had no success and had only spent money so far — no profits, no revenue even, only costs. After 2 weeks I got to a site named affbuzz. com. Affbuzz calls itself the 'affiliate marketing news aggregator.' They collect the latest and newest news articles and blog posts relating to affiliate marketing. Charles's articles were on there, as well as other big names in the industry. One post written by a guy named Ryan Buke really stood out to me. He had recently launched a one-stop shop for affiliate marketing. He had tracking software, an affiliate network, and a traffic source, called Bevo-Media. Apparently, Ryan had been doing this since he was fourteen years old. A little snooping on his blog showed that he had taught several people how to be profitable in the space. I sent him an email, using my best social skills.

What I'd learned from Jim, Joseph and Soul earlier that year about showing people respect would really come in handy.

*Dear Ryan,*

*I've come across your blog and wanted to send you an email saying how much I respect what you've done. It really looks like you've worked your ass off to get where you are.*

*I've also read that you've been able to help other people get started in the business.*

*That is something you can be very proud of as well!*

*If you have some time to talk one of these days, I'd love to be in touch!*

*Best regards,*
*Mark*

The next day I got an email back from him. He really appreciated me reaching out to him and told me to add him on Skype. I added him, but was too nervous to talk to him. Weeks went by, and we didn't even speak once.

One day I wanted to speak to a friend of mine who's also named Ryan, and by mistake I ended up talking to Ryan Buke.

'Hey man' he replied, 'so we finally talk.'

There was no way back from there. I had to chat with him now. We spoke about many things that day. About living in San Diego, about living in Poland, and about girls and clubs.

I told him I was nervous talking to him because I felt I should know a bit more about affiliate marketing before I did.

'That's stupid, bro' he said. 'Everyone always thinks that. Look man, you seem like a cool guy. If you really want to learn, I'll teach you, but it will take a real time commitment, and I'll charge $1k for a month of coaching.'

Whenever I speak to people about this now, they can't believe it. It all started with paying Ryan a thousand dollars.

The agreement was made. I would wake up every morning at 6 a.m. and would speak to him for about an hour. This was in the late evening for him, and it was very early in the morning for me. I knew it would be the same routine as always when I dove into something new, relentless studying and working, while enjoying the process. Enjoying the process is a key element, or you won't make it.

When talking to Ryan on Skype, I got to know him pretty well. He was short, a bit balding which he said was because he worked extremely hard. He wore glasses at night, during the day he wore contacts. The way he spoke was funny. He had a Californian surfer vibe in his voice.

His two favorite words were 'bro' and 'fresh.'

'Wassup, bro!?' is how he picked up the phone.

'Ah, that's fresh, bro!' Whenever he liked something and gave his approval.

'Zero fucks, bro!' When he didn't care, or admired someone for not caring.

'Hey Ryan, how are you doing?'

'Just living the dream, bro!' That was actually an activity for him it seemed, 'living the dream.'

Ryan was always in a good mood. It was astonishing how patient he was. Everything was funny to him. 'Yeah bro, I can't even imagine what someone would have to do to make me angry, bro. Why would I care? Life is fresh, bro. Zero fucks. Ship it!'

That was another thing he'd say, 'ship it!'

Ryan went to college. I didn't. When I asked him about it, he replied without letting me finish my sentence 'Oh, complete waste of time, bro! No, fuck that. Dumbest thing I've ever done. At least I got to play college football, that was fresh, bro!'

That's Ryan for you.

He explained to me how to research what I was promoting. He showed me how to 'spy' on other affiliates to get an idea of how they were promoting the same products. He showed me how to make a

Google AdWords account. You know those annoying ads on web-sites that follow you around the internet? 90% of those are from the Google AdWords network, and they make a shit ton of money.

'Yeah bro, so, on the internet there are companies like Groupon, airbnb, Amazon, and shit like that. These companies are looking to sell their products or services. Instead of doing their marketing themselves, or hiring an agency, they choose to pay a CPA, cost per acquisition, to their affiliates. So let's say you sell $100 in diet pills, the company then pays you a $50 CPA. Everybody wins. Now, as a professional affiliate marketer, it is your job to find a way to sell as many products as possible, as fast as you can, with as little costs as you can. That way you'll make the most money the fastest. It's tricky, bro, it's not easy. But once you find a good campaign that works, payoffs of $20k - $50k per day are possible. That's fucking fresh, bro. Believe me.'

He introduced me to an affiliate network that had denied me an account before, but this time they accepted me.

'What's funny about the affiliate marketing industry, every person on the planet is in touch with it several times each day. But no one knows it exists. When a user clicks on an ad that links to Amazon for example, and buys a product there, there are 4 more companies besides Amazon that make money on that transaction, and the end user never realizes this. There is the traffic source — the website the user is visiting. Then there is the company facilitating the adverts on that website, they auction that ad space in a split second to mil-lions of advertisers all over the world. Then there is the affiliate, like you, that buys that ad space and displays his advertisement. Then there is the affiliate network, they are a company that has relations with advertisers and companies that want to sell their products on-line. Then, finally, there is Amazon. Every step of the way a compa-ny makes money and the user never knows.'

After our talk, he went to sleep, and I went to work. I would literally work from 6 a.m. to midnight, go to sleep, wake up, drink a Red Bull, and repeat.

I'd only leave the apartment to go to the Subway downstairs to get food. I'd eat my food while I worked. During our talks, I made notes of everything he told me and the rest of the day would be spent researching everything, trying things out, and reading what he told me to read. I learned so much the first month; I don't think I've ever soaked up that much information that quickly.

'Affiliate marketing is like a computer game. You're constantly trying to get to the next level. Figure shit out to get you ahead. You're playing a computer game, and your bank account is your high score, bro.'

*Your bank account is your high score.*

# $2

The Love Systems super conference was coming up. It was a weekend in Las Vegas where all the instructors were going, and new instructors like me would get their assessment. This was held every year. It was a huge event with more than a thousand people. Love Systems rented half a floor of a hotel for their instructors, who went crazy in the clubs and casinos, picking up girls, getting drunk, and gambling.

The company paid for my ticket, and I'd get to meet the CEO. It was amazing. The lights of Las Vegas inspired me, flashing neon luring people in, lights dancing in time with fountains, and—behind it all—lights tricking gamblers into thinking there was never any time, or need, to sleep. There were tens of thousands of people partying, drinking, and having a good time everywhere I looked. The fountains of the Bellagio were spectacular, the water shot 460 feet in the air to the rhythm of the music. What a place to be for a street punk from small town Zwolle.

In one of the casinos, I walked over to a roulette table. A guy wearing a blue striped shirt, jeans and sneakers walked up and bought $5k worth of chips, then threw it all on a few numbers on the table. I watched his face as the wheel spun, and saw the agony in his eyes when it stopped. He'd lost it all. He clenched up, his face turned red and he shouted 'Fuck! Shit! Come on! Crap!' He bought another $5k worth of chips, did the same thing again, and lost. He turned around, stomped his feet, and cursed loudly. The waitress gave him a free drink. He sipped it, turned around, and bought another $5k worth of chips. He lost it again in one spin.

'Dammit! Dammit! Fuck this! Dammit!'

He walks to another table, and repeats.

That evening, all the instructors were meeting in the CEO's—Nick's—room. He was staying in a large suite. It had 2 bathrooms and 3 bedrooms. There was a bar in the room with a private bartender, who made us all the drinks we wanted. There was a 90-inch flat screen TV hanging on the wall, with two long blue sofas and 5 chairs on which the 27 instructors were seated in front of it. Jim was there, Soul, Chris and Cajun, as well as a whole bunch of guys I didn't know.

Nick asked me a string of questions about the theory.

'Alright, Mark, tell me, what does the Love Systems' model look like?'

'Well, uh... wait...' I stuttered.

'Are you nervous?' He asked.

'Yeah, kinda...'

'Ok, I'll get a drink, when I come back, I want my answer.'

He walked to the bar and ordered a gin and tonic. While he was gone I did my best to get a grasp on my thoughts. When he returned I started,

'Ok, so, there's the opener — What you say to her first. Then the transition — What you'll say next. Attraction — Get her attracted to you. Qualification — make sure she has the feeling she needs to qualify herself to you, make her work for it. Comfort — create enough comfort for sex to take place without it being awkward. Seduction — have sex with her.'

'Ok, that's great. How do you get a woman attracted to you?'

'There are basically eight attraction switches. Eight characteristics that women find attractive in men. Looks and health, Social intelligence, Humor, Social status, Wealth, Confidence, Pre-selection by other females — she needs to see that other women find you attractive, Congruence.'

'That's impressive.'

'What?'

'You're the first one to ever name them all by heart.'

I had studied the theory relentlessly.

He drilled me like this for an hour, then we went out to a club and he pointed out several women to me. I approached them to demonstrate my practical skills. It was tiring. I was still jet lagged and didn't feel 100-percent right. But I pulled through. It was an experience I'll never forget.

After the Super Conference, Jim, Charles, Laurent, a few students and I, went to Miami. We rented a huge villa with a swimming pool and shared the costs. Around this time, I had completed making my first marketing campaign with Ryan and was ready to launch.

It was a dating site I was promoting. They would pay me $5 per new user I brought them. I thought the dating niche would suit me because of my experience with Love Systems. We had created a website and a Google AdWords campaign to drive traffic to it. Ryan told me to activate the campaign and go to sleep. It would take a while to get traffic anyway.

When I woke up, I had spent $17.99 on traffic, and my revenue was $20....

A full $2 profit....

My. Mind. Was. Blown.

I opened my eyes as far as I could and stared at my computer screen. 'Oh my god, oh my god, oh my god...' I mumbled over and over.

I had made money online, and I was almost in disbelief. I saw now that it was possible to create things online that generated money. You could apparently make websites, and if you knew what you were doing, they would make you money.

Without Ryan's help, I would have never gotten there.

I spent the rest of the day sitting next to the pool just staring in the distance, fantasizing about how my life would change with this knowledge. I had made two dollars... online.

Charles told me it was literally the easiest marketing campaign there was and even an idiot could do it. I didn't mind. I'd be an idiot, an idiot who had made two dollars. Nothing was screwing up my mood. I was happy. I flew back to Europe with American Airlines. After landing in Berlin, I took the train from Ostbahnhof to Poznan. At the train station in Berlin my phone rang. It was a US number, starting with +1. I knew who it was.

'Hey, Mark, it's Nick here.'

The Love Systems' CEO was calling.

'Let me be the first to congratulate you and welcome you to the team. We all decided you have what it takes to be a Love Systems instructor.'

All the hard work had paid off, and I could call myself a Love Systems instructor now. This was something to be very proud of. My plans were no longer to instruct, though. I had plans of becoming an Internet millionaire. After all my experiences with Love Systems, it had given me the knowledge and confidence to know that anything can be achieved. It's all possible. The $2 I had made were proof of that. Countless times I had heard people say that things can't be done, but they can. Those are all limiting beliefs. Things we tell ourselves, things we believe, that aren't true, and limit what we believe is possible. We are all capable of more things than we can imagine.

I was determined to see how far I could take this.

# CHANGING LIVES

Even with an increased focus on building campaigns, I still managed to help out at bootcamps in several cities around Europe and in the United States as well. I wasn't able to be as active as other instructors, but there was one aspect of being an instructor with Love Systems that I couldn't get enough of.

I had the opportunity to change lives.

The feeling I got from having an impact on someone's life, a positive impact, is what made it all worthwhile for me. Every student who came in was transformed from a socially awkward, insecure guy into someone who knew he could get anything he wanted if he changed his behavior.

Change your behavior, and you'll change your results.

I stood tall behind a dark wooden desk in front of a room of students.

'Alrighty guys, let's get started. I'll make this simple.' The seminar began.

I turned around, picked up a green marker, and wrote on the white board.

NICE. DOMINANT. SEXUAL.

'The Love Systems theory is very long and difficult to remember. Especially when in a club approaching a girl you don't know. It's way too much information to have in your head. So I created my own little system of three things to remember while I'm out: Be nice, Be dominant, Be sexual. That is it. If I'll do those three things right, the majority of women will be attracted to me. This is what guys who are naturally attractive to women do already. They don't have to put in any effort, it's just the way they are.'

I glanced around the room, full of nervous men smiling timidly, and continued.

'In practice, this means; smile, stand up straight, give compliments, don't be too eager, hold open doors, dress nice, lead the interaction, touch.'

I lifted my chin up and pushed my shoulders back. 'Oh, and the entire time,' I raised my voice, 'never forget to STAND TALL and SPEAK UP!' I smiled while I looked down on them.

Whenever I could, I reminded students they were just a regular guy, talking to a regular girl.

'You're not 'trying' to sleep with her, you're not 'trying' to show her how cool you are, you're not trying anything. No matter how beautiful or special you think she is, she is just a regular girl just like any other, and you are just a regular guy, just like any other.' I raised my eyebrows and smiled.

'If your frame of mind is strong, everyone will play along.'

I sat down on the edge of the desk. 'Don't expect anything from the interaction. Don't be attached to any outcome. The real intentions are always shining through. If you have a hidden agenda, she will pick up on it. But, if you have the frame of mind that you are just a guy talking to a girl, without any intentions besides just seeing if she is a good person to have a conversation with, you just assume she is attracted to you anyway and you do not need to win her over or prove anything to her, the interaction will be smooth. She'll feel like she's convincing you of her qualities, instead of the other way around.'

A man with glasses and a long red beard held his hand high up in the air.

'Uh, what do you mean by, 'be nice'? My whole problem is that I'm too nice. I'm always the 'nice guy' and never the 'attractive guy' I thought I wasn't supposed to be nice?'

'Ok, most people, including women, think there are only two types of men. The 'nice guys', who they categorize as unattractive pussies. No offense. Or the confident guys, the attractive guys, who are basically always assholes. But, there is a third type of man. This one is way rarer, but also way more attractive to most women. The confident, sexually aggressive, nice guy. Most women have never encountered such a man. A man who is honest about his intentions, a man who can have any woman he desires, but does not act like an asshole because of it. His niceness will accentuate his confidence. That is what a true leader is, and it is very attractive.'

The room filled with the sound of scribbling, dozens of pens scratching paper simultaneously. I knew they were with me.

'These three don't work separate from each other. You'll need all of them. Look at the other two factors: Be dominant. Be sexual.' I pointed at the white-board. 'You can't be a dominant, sexual asshole to women you've just met. You'll probably be arrested. Throw 'nice' into the mix and you'll get way better results.'

'Ok, so when you say that we should be dominant, how does that fit into being nice? It seems contradictory,' said the same guy.

'Dominance can be as minimal as taking control of a social situation. Most of the time, just the approach itself can portray dominance. Just the demonstration that you are the type of man that walks up to a woman and tells her what he wants is dominant enough. This will be enhanced if, at the same time, you show enough social intelligence to create enough comfort so the situation won't get awkward and everyone feels at ease.'

Ah yes, that makes sense' he said and wrote it all down. I pointed at the word SEXUAL.

'Sexuality can be easily demonstrated by showing the right body language and touching her at the right places at the right time. I'd usually start with a slight touch on the inside of her arm, or around her wrist. These are both erogenous zones, but not too threatening, and socially acceptable for someone you've just met. Don't touch for too long, but not too briefly either. Taking away the touch is just as important, so she can have the feeling of missing it. After this, you can go a step further, like put your hand on her waist, but take it back shortly after. Move in close to her with your hips at the right time, but, just as importantly, move away at the right time. Build tension! Escalate the touches by taking one step back and two steps forward, all the way until - and during - sex.'

'Well, that's usually where I get nervous. Haha, that's the scariest part. Where things are going well, and then I'll have to kiss her. I mean, she usually turns her head away and I stand there feeling like an idiot. It's over for me then.'

'You're wrong about that. That's when it's just getting started! The moment where I know I have her, is when I go in for the kiss, and she turns her head away. This is usually the situation that guys are terrified of, because they see this as a rejection. But I know it is not a rejection. It's a 'not yet', not a 'no.' Just continue like nothing had happened. Don't get nervous because of this; if you do, you blow it. If you get nervous, she'll think that she was wrong about you. She thought you were confident, but then why would you get nervous? Just continue like nothing happened. If you just keep doing what you've been doing all along, and she keeps giving you the same signs, she literally told you 'I want you to kiss me, we will kiss, not now, but it is going to happen, 100-percent sure!' If she was not attracted to you at all, she would leave. If she is still there, her sub-communications are telling you that she has accepted your intentions, and she is fine with it.'

Every face was staring at me.

'Look,' I continued, 'Anything she does to you that you would not do to a gay guy in a gay club means that she is attracted to you.'

Several students leaned forward.

'If you're a heterosexual man, and for some reason you end up in a gay bar, and a gay man walks up to you and starts a conversation, how long would you hold his hand after shaking it? Would you touch him while talking? Would you follow him to a quiet corner to talk more intimately? Would you still talk to him like nothing happened after he tried kissing you?'

The room burst out in laughter.

'If he walks up to you and says, 'Hey, I think you are absolutely handsome and I just had to come and talk to you, or I'd regret it.' Would you talk to him? You'd most likely do none of those things. If she does any of them, she is attracted to you. Any questions?'

There were no questions.

'Great, now, for sex to take place, there needs to be two equally important emotions in her.'

I turned back to the whiteboard. ATTRACTION. COMFORT.

'She needs to be attracted to you so that she has a sexual interest. She needs to be comfortable enough with you in order for sex to take place without it being awkward. Some women need more comfort than others, and some women are more easily attracted than others. This will be determined on a case-by-case basis, and is measured by the amount of compliance she is showing through her body language. It's not what she says, but what she does. The problem with attraction and comfort is that they're often at war with each other. The more comfortable she is with you, the less attracted she will be. We all know the dreaded 'friend zone,' where a girl likes a guy a lot, but there is no physical attraction.'

I looked at the student with the red beard, and he was slowly nodding his head.

'This is a classic example of creating too much comfort, without creating any attraction. It's very difficult for a woman to feel attracted to a man after this has been established. This is why it is very important to first create attraction. As soon as you see the physical signs of attraction, that's when you can start building comfort. But, you cannot start getting comfortable right away, because then the attraction will fade away. There is a balancing act you need to get good at. This is where 'take aways' come in. After establishing attraction, you pretend you're moving away from her. You let go of her touch. Or even literally tell her, while smiling, 'What did you say?? Oh I don't like you anymore!' and turn your back toward her. As soon as you see her putting in effort to win you back, that's when you turn around with a big smile and say something like 'Ohhh, OK I forgive you!' and give her a big hug. Now you've spiked attraction, and built more comfort, in a very, very smooth way. This is an example, it all depends on the type of woman you're talking to, and the situation you're in. The 'Attract - Take Away - Build Comfort - Repeat' model will always be there, but it will take different forms when talking to a sophisticated woman in a restaurant and a high-energy, twenty-something girl in a club.'

After the seminar we went out to the clubs, where the other instructors and I showed them how to put this theory into practice.

We changed lives.

# AMSTERDAM

I was in a Club in Amsterdam called Paradiso with a student named Christian. We had known each other for a while. I was in town for one night and was sleeping on his sofa. We decided to go out to meet some women.

From the corner of my eye I saw a short blonde girl with long black eyelashes, and listened as she ordered a drink in English. She was with a man.

I waited until she turned around, touched her elbow, and loudly said, 'Hi!' like I knew her. I turned to the guy she was with and told him, 'Just a minute!' as if saying 'don't worry, I just need to ask her something.' He thought I knew her, so it's the polite thing to do to let me speak to her and don't interrupt.

She looked up at me with a smile, 'Hey.'

I leaned in close, so close we could sense each other's body heat through our almost touching cheeks. 'I actually saw you when you came in.... I wanted to speak to you before... I think you are adorable... I just had to come and meet you... Hi, my name is Mark.'

After I said this I leaned back and kept eye contact. She looked at me surprised and intrigued, then shook my hand and introduced herself. I held her hand, turned her around, and leaned back against the bar, giving myself a comfortable position, and making her face away from the man she was with. I continued talking to her.

'So where are you from?'

'I'm from Sydney.'

'Oh shit....' I said, smiling. I leaned into her and told her '...my mom warned me about girls from Sydney, you must be trouble..' I leaned back and looked in her eyes. She grinned and briefly looked at my lips. Then back in my eyes.

That guy she was with stood there. He couldn't figure out what to do. It was clear to me it was not her boyfriend by the way he was doubting how to handle the situation. I needed to keep her mind occupied, so he wouldn't get any more attention and would understand it was best if he left.

She wore a white long dress that accentuated her figure. Her breasts were large and they touched me when she leaned in to speak.

'Where are you from?' she asked me, while touching me below my shoulder with the palm of her hand, a clear sign of attraction.

I told her to guess. She guessed wrong, and then I confessed I was a local. She told me that she studied management and I teased her that that probably made her very bossy, and we would probably not get along at all.

'I'm not as bossy as you might think,' she said while giving me a little push. The guy she was with left.

'Ok, so what is it that you do in normal life besides studying?'

'I organize parties for people that are into extreme sports.'

'Have you ever sky dived?' I asked her.

'No I haven't, but I've always wanted to.'

'Me too. We should do it together! I've bungee jumped though, but you know, it's not the same rush. With skydiving, you can't see the parachute inside, and it might not even open, but with bungee jumping you can see the cord attached to your feet, you know nothing will happen, I feel a lot safer like that.'

She started laughing. 'Oh my god! How did I stumble on to you!?' She looked at me in awe.

'You are too cute! Give me a hug and shut up!' I told her and hugged her, then pushed her away.

'Ok get off me, you! I'm not that easy!'

While we were talking, we were touching each other back and forth. I said something and touched her waist, then pushed her away as I teased her. She pulled me back.

'Do you have any brothers or sisters?' I asked.

'I had a brother, but he died.'

'Yeah, I knew that... I can just tell...'

'What do you mean?'

'Well, you have this cute innocent little sister vibe around you, but you come of as someone who has been taking care of herself for a while now; it has toughened you up.'

This honestly was the feeling she gave me. It just made sense.

'Yeah, you know... that is exactly me.'

The guy she was with earlier came back and started a conversation with her. I waited five seconds, then looked at them both and asked,

'How do you two know each other?'

This put a lot of pressure on him, and I felt it. What will she say? Is what he was thinking. 'Oh we don't know each other' she replied. 'We just met today.'

Perfect

'Let's go over here,' I said, 'Let me introduce you to my buddy. He is a great guy. You'll like him,' and grabbed her hand to lead her away.

I introduced her to Christian, 'Meet my best friend!'

Christian shook her hand, 'Hi I'm Chris, nice to meet you. How do you know Mark? Let me tell you, this guy is AMAZING!'

'Haha, really?'

'Yeah, really, he is the best person I know.'

She looked over at me and me and smiled big. I grabbed her wrist loosely and led her to the floor where we danced. We moved around the venue. I leaned against a pillar and watched as she moved herself, trying to turn me on.

'You're turning me on,' I told her.

'Oh am I...?' she asked with a mischievous smile while turning around and moving her ass against me. It gave me an erection.

I pressed her hand between my legs for one second, then pushed her away.

'But you're gonna have to work harder for it, I'm not there yet.'

She smiled and pushed her breasts against me.

'I'm not going home with you. You can forget it!'

So she actually was considering going home with me. No need to worry.

I knew she needed more comfort. The attraction was there, but the comfort was lacking. I had learned that comfort equals time, plus shared experiences. If I'd give her the feeling we spent more time together, and shared more experiences, she would go home with me. I grabbed her hand. 'Come with me,' I said and took her to the bar. Then I took her to the other side of the club. Then back to the dance floor, all the while talking, keeping her entertained. The more places you take her; the more experiences she feels you have had together. Our mind plays tricks on us like that.

We kissed and made out. While staring into her eyes, I told her 'Oh my god, I don't know what it is, I don't even know you but I just have this feeling.... you are so sexy; you make me wanna fuck you... but you just give me the feeling like I have to take care of you...'

She hugged me.

I looked at my watch. 'Shit, I have an early flight in the morning. I'm actually going to London.' I had to teach in London the next day, I honestly forgot because the night was going so well.

'Oh really?' she asked, disappointed.

'Yes, I gotta go, and you're coming with me, get your coat!' I grabbed her hand and walked with her to the exit. We spent the night together on Christian's sofa. The next morning, I got up early. She went to her hotel, I went to the airport.

We never spoke again.

# EFFORTS BEING NOTICED

The following day, Jim, Soul, and I were teaching a bootcamp in London. I took a few students to my favorite place to teach in London; Jewel bar, on Piccadilly Circus.

Jewel bar is a central London venue with a dark grey ceiling and long glass chandeliers. It has a dark wooden floor, and a 5-steps staircase separating the dance floor from the bar area. I sat down on one of the purple velvet sofas with three of the students.

A student named Phill, wearing a T-shirt and a blazer, asked me to do a demonstration of a direct approach.

'Pick a woman,' I said.

He looked at me, surprised, then scanned the bar. 'What about her?' He pointed at a black haired woman in her late twenties. She was standing in a circle of women, on the side of the dance floor. She wore glasses. Her grey jacket had no sleeves, it was held together with a beige belt, and reached down to her knees. Her lipstick was bright red and, even from across the bar, the marks it left on her champagne glass were evident. The whole group of women were dressed business-casual. Some of them carried small suitcases. Next to the group was a table. On that table was an ice bucket with the logo Moët & Chandon on it, in it a bottle of champagne. The women were talking and laughing. They only had eyes for each other, and were quite engaged. 'Ok, good choice' I told him, and started walking toward her. This was a horrible situation. She was surrounded by women, who might be her friends, but could also be her co- workers or family, even.

Women usually 'protect' each other from men that are bothering them, or get jealous when their friends get attention and they don't. This put extra pressure on me, her, and the people she was with. It's a terrible situation to be in, and a recipe for awkwardness.

Because I would not allow myself to have any second thoughts, I started moving toward her immediately after the student pointed her out. If I'd allow myself to think about the situation, I would come up with every possible reason not to do it. However, by walking toward her, the approach was already set in motion, and there was no way back.

I slightly touched the inside of her elbow with two fingers. 'Hi!' I said, with the same upbeat tonality and expression I would have when greeting an old friend I had not seen in awhile. This gave the whole group the feeling like I knew her. Now they would not see me as an intruder. 'Hey!' She said back, with a smile like she was trying to figure out where she knew me from. I turned to face the entire group, created eye contact with all the women, stood up straight, leaned slightly back, chin up, and smiled.

'I'm sorry guys, but I just HAVE TO speak to your friend for a bit, is that OK?'

This was a rhetorical question. I asked it to the entire group so that they would feel respected and at ease. Her friends have to know what's going on, it's girl code to keep an eye on each other.

'Oh sure, go ahead!' a few women replied.

Now I had gotten the approval of the group she was with, giving me social proof and making her comfortable with my presence. I grabbed her wrist loosely, led her a few steps away, and turned her so she was facing away from the group and looking into my eyes. This way we'd have no distractions.

'I was just standing over there with my friend,' I pointed at Phill, 'and then I saw you... I thought you were absolutely gorgeous... and I knew I'd be kicking myself if I didn't come up to you and say hi...' Her eyes sparkled and she smiled.

'My name is Mark. Nice to meet you.' I looked into her eyes while leaning back against a wall. She introduced herself, she grabbed my hand loosely.

'Hi, I'm Patricia.'

Our fingers locked, and I asked, 'Where are you from?'

'I am from London.'

I looked over at her friends, then back at her.

'So, are you guys in a circus or something?'

'Hahaha what?! No! I'm a lawyer, and these are my co-workers!' She punched my arm.

'What, a shady lawyer? No way, I can't talk to you anymore!' I said while smiling and turned my back to her. She grabbed my arm and tried to pull me back. I turned back to her and smiled.

'Ok, ok, what's the occasion here?' I asked while moving my hand to her upper arm. 'You seem like you guys are having a party of some sort.' I let go of her arm and did a small step back.

She held my wrist and leaned in to speak, 'We just finished one of the biggest cases I've ever worked on, and it went great for us.' She smiled at me, proud.

'Oh you guys got an orphanage foreclosed, and you're celebrating? Yeah that makes sense.' I said while smiling and nodding as if I just figured her out.

'Haha stop it you!' She pushed me.

'No, actually that's great, give me a high five!' I held my hand up. She looked at it, then quickly high-fived me, and held her hand against mine. Our fingers locked again. I turned her around like a ballerina, put my arm around her waist, I lifted her up, turned 360 degrees, and put her down again. Then, I kissed her.

She looked at me, 'Now I know that Dutch guys are just as smooth as Londoners.'

We exchanged numbers and I told her she might want to rejoin her friends. I looked over at Phill and his jaw was on the floor. We walked to a more remote corner and I explained to him exactly what I did and why I did it. His life was changed forever.

While in Oslo, we had a student named Gavin who flew from Berlin. He was a short, cute looking fellow of Indian descent. He was a bit shy, wore glasses, and dressed kind of nerdy. I liked him immediately. What a delightful character he was; so polite.

We went into a club in the city center and I pointed out a girl to him. He walked to her, a bit hunched over, with a look on his face like he was expecting her to reject him, and she did. I explained to him what he did wrong and showed him how to do it. I walked over to the same girl, back straight, chin slightly up, strong eye contact, big smile.

'Hi! I just had to come and talk to you!'

'Oh really? Why?'

'I think you are drop dead gorgeous and I at least had to come over here and meet you. Hi, my name is Mark.'

I wasn't wasting time here, I just wanted to show Gavin how it's done. She looked at me with a smile that showed me she was impressed. She shook my hand and held it a bit longer while looking into my eyes. We spoke briefly, then I told her I really had to go back to my friends and gave her a small kiss on the lips.

'Ok, but I hope I'll see you again?'

'Maybe...' I replied.

Gavin looked like he'd seen with his own eyes what he had been doing wrong all of his life. I pointed to a tall blonde Norwegian girl in a sexy pink dress and told him to go for it. He was hesitant.

'No, man, she is too hot. Ugh, my god, no I can't.'

'Gavin, I want you to understand something.' I firmly grabbed his right shoulder, and made strong eye contact with him. 'You are an alpha male! It's a privilege for her to talk to you! Now walk over there like this is your house and she came here to visit you. Be a good host and talk to her. You own this place!'

His body language turned confident, just like I'd showed him. He approached the girl just like I did before, and it immediately became clear she was intrigued. Her first reaction was to smile, she shook his hand slowly while looking in his eyes, her other hand over her breasts with spread fingers. She leaned into him while he spoke, he leaned back.

After a while, I could see that she wanted him to kiss her. She kept moving in closer with her face, looking at his lips briefly before turning her gaze back into his eyes, waiting for him to make the move. But poor Gavin had never experienced this. He had no clue. Gavin looked away nervously each time she did this. It was a matter of time before she would be disappointed and lose interest. When it comes to romance, as a man you need to know when to move forward, or you'll lose the girl.

I Introduced myself to her. 'Hi, I'm Mark.' She shook my hand. 'I can see you are talking to my best friend Gavin here, but I don't know if you're cool enough to speak to him to be honest.' She looked a bit shocked, 'Yes I am!'

'Ok fine... but... I bet... you're... a... lousy... kisser.' I put up a little challenge for her.

'No, I'm a GREAT kisser!' she replied.

'Alright, I'm gonna give you one chance to prove it, but only one, OK? If you blow it, it's over. You two will kiss for three seconds, and then Gavin will tell me if that's true.'

Gavin kissed her immediately. I don't think I've ever seen anyone that eager to kiss. Now a short, nerdy, Indian boy was making out with the hottest girl in the club. The next day he was radiating confidence. I loved it. This is what really made me happy.

Some people back in Zwolle heard what I was doing. One of them told a local magazine about it and I received a phone call. The editor asked if I would be willing to give an interview. They published a two-page story about me titled Dating Doctor Mark V and The Art of Seduction.

After this article was published, I got emails, phone calls, and Facebook messages from people back home. The difference in the world we now lived in became very clear.

It felt good to me that something I was doing was getting noticed back home, because most people in Zwolle had absolutely no idea what my life currently looked like. I spent some time talking to people and catching up.

# A FRIEND REQUEST

I was out in a club in Poznan with Gucio, Anthony, and Bartek. We sat on one of the white leather sofas next to the dance floor when my attention was grabbed by three girls at the bar. They did not look like the average, club going women. They were dressed with more class.

One girl in particular wore a red dress, with red high heels. She had long black eye lashes, thick red lips, shiny blonde hair, and was holding a cosmopolitan. I found her to be very pretty, sexy, slim with round curves, and dressed with taste. The girls were talking to each other, while pointing out people in the room and laughing.

The girl in red looked in my direction. We held eye contact briefly, I felt my face blushing, then she returned her attention back to the other girls and started laughing again.

*Should I talk to her? I probably should.* I thought to myself. *I've done this many times before. Why do I feel like this?* Approach anxiety is an irrational fear that does not go away. It makes no difference how experienced you are; the fear of approaching unknown women is hardwired in our DNA.

*Fuck it. Let's go.*

'Alright guys, I need to go talk to her. I'll be right back.'

I walked over to the bar, placed myself next to the girl in red, and ordered a drink. I turned my head and looked at her. She ignored me, just looked straight ahead, as if I was not there.

*Weird.*

'Hi!' I said while touching the inside of her elbow. She gave no re-action. She kept looking in front of her as if she did not notice me. I leaned into her, 'I was standing over there with my friends... and I ...' The girls walked away in the middle of my sentence.

I was left standing at the bar, by myself, looking at the girls as they moved toward another part of the room, making me look like a complete idiot. I felt the whole club was looking at me. 'What the fuck...' I mumbled to myself, angry. Frustrated.

The bar tender was laughing. Gucio, Anthony, and Bartek were laughing. I looked back at the girls. They were laughing.

I felt like an idiot. *Where does this chick get the nerve? She could at least say something. What a fucking bitch.* I felt so small.

I sat down next to the guys, who were still giggling. 'Fuck off guys. I don't care.' I sipped my vodka and coke. Shortly after this I went home. I wasn't feeling it anymore.

The next morning, while drinking orange juice in my underwear behind my desk, I received a Facebook friend request from a girl named Stefania. I accepted it.

'Holy fucking shit. What?' I whispered to myself, after looking at her pictures. It was the blonde girl in red, from the night before.

'Hey.' She started a chat. 'I saw you in the club yesterday. Do you live in Poznan?'

When I tried to speak to this girl she looked through me like I was made out of air. It was the worst shut-down I'd ever experienced. Now she was talking to me as if nothing happened. *What is she up to?*

'Sometimes.' I replied. 'I just got back from Oslo.'

'What are you doing in Poland?'

'Just for work,' I lied, and continued, 'So, are you like stalking me now, or something?' I tried to tease her.

'What do you mean? Don't be stupid.'

'I was just joking.' *Am I really explaining myself to her?*

'Oh, that wasn't funny.'

*I need to change the subject.*

'I don't have much time to talk now,' I continued. 'But I am planning on going out later for lunch. if you're in the area you can drop by if you want, but now I gotta go.'

*That will buy me some time at least.*

I wasn't going there really. I wanted to see her, but I didn't want to seem too eager. I said I was going there anyway, and if she would be willing to show up, I would have some time to fit her into my busy schedule. But I didn't really care. That was how I presented it. I hoped she bought it.

'Ok, I might come.' She replied.

Stefania couldn't believe I took her to that restaurant. It was most likely the shittiest kebab place in town. I figured she deserved that after the stunt she pulled in the club the night before. It looked as if I was not trying to impress her at all, and it gave me lots of room to make the evening better if things went well. By planning to be a bit late, I made sure she was already inside when I arrived.

She had long, glossy blonde hair and wore a tight grey dress that ended slightly above her knees. It showed modest cleavage, enough to draw my eyes in. Her breasts were large and round. She wore a light pink lipstick which made her lips seem full and shiny. She took great care of her appearance, I could tell.

Lots of times when you meet a gorgeous woman in a club, her looks are disappointing when you meet her the next day in the daylight. Stefania's weren't. She looked even more stunning than the night before.

I entered the restaurant. She sat up straight, held her hand at shoulder height, and waved at me by quickly moving her four fingers separate from each other.

'Hey, oh... you are here already? I didn't expect that.' I said while I gave her a kiss on the cheek and sat down next to her.

'Yes, and you're late. I don't like that.'

'Well, that's too bad then, missy.' I replied in a dominant tone. She smiled and her eyes pierced straight through me.

The waiter came over and placed two plates with cutlery on the table. Stefania grabbed her fork, held it against the light. Then grabbed my fork and did the same.

'Excuse me!' She said to the waiter while he walked away. 'Could you bring us clean cutlery please, these are dirty.' The waiter looked surprised and he walked back to our table.

'...and please make sure they are clean this time.' She handed him the knives and forks and smiled at him sarcastically. He looked at the forks, doing his best to detect anything dirty on them.

I leaned back in my chair, placing my arm behind the arm rest, 'You must be the bossiest girl in Poland.'

'If everyone would tell them to clean their dishes better, they would have cleaner dishes.'

'You got a point there.' I smiled and nodded, doing my best to look goofy.

'Besides, everyone knows I'm a bitch. I don't care.'

'So, where are you from?' I asked.

'Warsaw,' she replied, while lighting up a slim cigarette. In Poland you were still allowed to smoke in restaurants around that time.

We had long conversations. Stefania came from a wealthy family. She lived with her Parents in Warsaw, but spent most of her time at her Aunt and Uncle's, who lived in a villa in Poznan.

'So, what the fuck was that yesterday? You're too good to talk to me in a club?'

'I pick the men I date. Men don't pick me.' She said while looking very strict. 'I don't care who you are, I am not the type of girl that gets picked up in a club. I'm not some slut.'

'Oh, I never call girls sluts.' I replied.

'But I do.'

With her it was hard to lead the interaction, but I was doing my best.

Every guy in the restaurant couldn't help but look over at her every few seconds through the corners of their eyes, even the ones there with their girlfriends.

At home I had already checked what movies were playing in the cinema. The new Sex and the City movie just came out. It was the perfect chick flick to get her in the mood.

'If you promise to behave yourself, we can go to the cinema later.' I told her.

'I don't have to promise you anything, but I'll go with you.' She placed her cigarette in the ashtray, and got her coat. 'Are you coming?' She smirked as she walked to the door. I felt there was a power struggle going on between us.

After the movie ended, I grabbed her hand and told her, 'We are going to my place. I'm going to cook for you.' I didn't give her a choice. We went to my apartment after doing some grocery shopping first. Grocery shopping with women creates a certain frame. It seems very casual, as if you're not trying, and it is something couples do together. Subconsciously, it creates a bond.

When we entered my apartment, she looked around. The empty cans on the table with cigarette butts in them. A plate with weed in the middle. Rolling papers, dirty socks and underwear, books, and other clutter was spread out over the floor.

'How dare you bring a lady here?'

'What? You don't like my place?'

'Someone has to clean this mess.' She said, determined, while she glanced through the room.

I cooked her the exact same dish I always cooked for girls, pasta with tomato sauce and garlic. When I finished I entered my living room, and it was spotless. All dirty clothes were in the washing machine, all clutter was gone, the floor was mopped. She even organized the books on my bookshelf, and spread out an Ikea carpet I had thrown in the corner—still in its original packaging—across the floor.

'Wow, what did you do?'

'Someone had to do it, apparently, Mark. You have no clue. I'm not eating in that mess, who do you think I am?' She said with a smile, while she held her fork and looked at the food.

'Hmm, that looks delicious.'

After we ate I told her 'get your shoes,' giving her no choice again, and we went to a club where Gucio was playing. Inside, a guy I had seen around before walked up to me and shouted in my ear,

'Holy shit, dude. She looks smoking! Look at those boobs! It's unbelievable!' I pushed him away.

'What did that guy tell you?' She asked me.

'Uhh... He was admiring your dress.'

'Oh, thank you,' she told him. I chuckled.

We danced around the room while Gucio spun his records. We drank shots of vodka and tequila. Hours later after the club closed, we frolicked through the city center streets, made out after every few steps, and eventually ended up in my apartment again.

I threw her on the sofa. We had long, amazing sex. Because my curtains were wide open I wondered if any neighbors saw us. She didn't seem to mind at all.

The reactions she gave me were different than any other girl. She did not let me tease her, she was doing her best to stay in control, and she was admittedly really good at it. She had her own will and confidence unlike any other girl I ever came across, and I loved it.

Beneath her tough exterior, I found a sweet and caring person. When she left the next day, she had a tear in her eye.

'What's wrong?' I asked her.

'This was the best date of my life,' she told me.

'Mine too,' I answered, looked deeply in her eyes for a few seconds, and gave her a long kiss. She smiled at me over her shoulder as she walked down the stairs. I was amazed by her. I really fell in love.

We dated for a few months, then she moved in.

# NO CHALLENGE

The whole Dating scene started to annoy me. A few things were clear to me that weren't when I started. I had learned it was no big deal to walk over to any woman and start a conversation. As long as she is a normal person without too many deep emotional problems, or isn't in a terrible mood for personal reasons, she would most likely at least have a conversation with me.

Because I had done nothing else than work on my sub-communications for the past year and a half and studied how attraction is created, the obvious result was that she would become attracted to me, even if it was just a little. Women are looking for men. That is something a lot of students didn't, and don't, understand.

Women want to meet men.

You're not selling them anything they don't want or need. It's the whole reason why they are out. They want to meet a nice, attractive, well-behaved man. 'Well-behaved' can mean different things to different women. But my point is, you're not doing anything special. If you're not a complete weirdo, chances are, women want to sleep with you anyway.

So why is this an accomplishment? I got bored with it — no challenge. I also got sick of students looking up to me for acting normally. I wasn't performing a trick. This is who I really am. I had learned new behavior, yes, but all our behavior is learned, and at some point it becomes part of us. We, us, define who we are.

This behavior was now who I was naturally. I couldn't help it. When I picked up a girl, it felt like I was a highly skilled psychologist who was taking advantage of his emotionally unstable patients. These girls had no clue. They weren't trained in this the way I was. They were following their emotions, and I was able to predict how they'd respond. It felt as if I was taking advantage. It felt immoral. I was no longer enjoying myself.

Besides that, a lot of people started to misunderstand and misuse what we were teaching. A lot of angry, socially awkward guys, who had been getting rejected most of their lives, saw our teachings as a way of having their revenge on women. That was the opposite of what it was intended for, and I wanted nothing to do with it. The whole thing became a joke to me.

This experience had taught me that anything could be achieved. I am very grateful and very happy that I dedicated a few years of my life to this. It taught me very valuable lessons about myself and other people. We're all the fucking same. No matter where we're born, or how tall we are, or what our culture or family looks like... we're all people. Even the ~~assholes~~ people from Zwolle.

Everywhere I went, people said things like, 'Oh I can't do that.' Or even, 'That won't work on the girls from (enter any country you'd like).' But you can, and it will. People are not so different as you might think.

I've learned that my abilities, and the abilities of others, are endless. I can recommend it to anybody. I've changed my own behavior and gotten different results. Not only that, but I taught those same behaviors to others, and they got similar results, too.

I mastered love. I mastered one night stands. I mastered human relationships. What else is out there that I can master? What else do I think can't be done, but it can? Just like I managed to fill my life with beautiful women, I can fill my bank account with money.

That's the next challenge. Time for the next phase of my life. This one is over.

# WHAT'S YOUR HIGH SCORE?

*W*hat is a normal amount of money to make each day? Is it a hundred dollars? Two hundred? Why not a thousand? Why not a million? Why not ten million? I'm just saying. They are just numbers. They add to your high score, that's it. Nothing more than that. Normal, is an empty word.

Normal is just something you're telling yourself. It doesn't exist. You should not be normal. Fuck being normal. Normal is an insult. If you tell yourself it's normal to make a hundred grand a day or one dollar a day, then that is normal. You are the one that decides that.

Someone will make that money, it might as well be you. That money is going to end up in someone's bank account. You have a bank account. It might as well end up in yours. Everything you can come up with that prevents you from making millions of dollars is some bullshit story you tell yourself.

# FACEBOOK ADS

I Stayed in Poznan for a while, living with Stefania in my apartment in the center. It was a nice change of pace for me. I had everything I needed at home, and it gave me all the time that was necessary to focus on building my online marketing skills.

My campaign on Google AdWords continued to make higher profits each day. My best day was $50. Then, one day, my cost per click went through the roof, and my traffic stopped.

I panicked. *What the fuck is going on?* Ryan explained to me that Google does this whenever a campaign receives complaints or they find out you're doing anything against their guidelines. Bummer.

I asked Ryan if we couldn't do a campaign on Facebook ads. I believed that's what Charles was doing. Ryan showed me how to make advertisements on Facebook. I started by promoting a company called Quality Health, in the US. On the spy tools Ryan had shown me, I found other affiliates promoting that campaign. I copied their ads. After I played around a bit with the age targeting on the Facebook platform, I managed to get cheaper clicks, and the campaign became profitable. I started doing $300 profit a day, then $500, eventually $2000 in one day. I couldn't believe it. This was so much money.

When I started making these amounts of money, it started feeling very uncomfortable. It's like vertigo. You are up so high, probably nothing will happen but the height just makes you woozy and scared you might fall. The same thing happened to me when I started making serious amounts of cash. It's all in your head, you have to get used to this.

After a week, they shut me down. Quality Health said my leads were not performing well for them. People were subscribing, but then they weren't spending any money.

I opened up ten accounts at different affiliate networks that had the same offer after Ryan advised me to do this and started doing $300 a day in profit on all of them to fly under the radar. This actually worked. This way I made $3000 per day profit for a while, until eventually all those accounts were shut down.

Ryan said, 'It's all part of the game, bro. As an affiliate marketer, this is the bullshit you gotta deal with. It's nothing compared to the hassle you get from running a supermarket or something. Those profits are lower and it's way more hassle dealing with employees' bullshit, bro. You don't have to deal with shit except Facebook and affiliate campaigns. That's fresh, bro, trust me.'

By this time, I had $50k in the bank, but I did not allow myself to spend it. I kept my regular routine of working from 6 a.m. until midnight, only leaving the house to eat, and I wasn't spending any money on anything. This discipline was needed to make it in this business. I had learned that from Charles.

I got a Skype call from my account manager at Neverblue, a Canadian affiliate network, one of the biggest in the business.

'Hey Mark, Groupon is launching in the Netherlands, and they are looking for 50k leads per month in that country. Is this something you could do? It should be easy for you because you speak Dutch.'

He showed me the page, and users had to fill out a three-field form.

Name, Email, Password.

That was it. If they'd do that Groupon would pay me $2. There are 17 million people living in the Netherlands, which gave me lots of room to make lots of money. I translated my ads to Dutch myself, created an advertising account with a site in the Netherlands, and did a 100-euro test. My revenue was $250. It worked, I started to make several thousand per day in revenue. I launched the same campaign on different websites, and I did an average of $150k revenue per month, half of which was profit.

Roan had gone on his own path of self-improvement by then. He also experienced that Zwolle was a terrible environment to live in because of the history we had there. He moved to Nijmegen, about 60-mile drive from Zwolle. At first, he was planning on going to University there, but he soon figured out he hated that. After that, he spent his entire time partying and using drugs. Old habits died hard for all of us. Soon, he had burned through all his money and needed to find a job, fast. I offered to loan him some cash to cover his living expenses. He really appreciated it, and he took it very seriously. He promised to pay me back as soon as he could. He got a temporary job at ASML, the world's biggest company producing machines that build microchips. They owned 80 percent of the world's market and are located in Eindhoven, a twenty-minute drive from Nijmegen. He learned how to code like a pro there. They soon realized he was one of their best guys and gave him a full-time job. He earned a decent living and drove a company Lexus — a pretty sweet deal. Roan paid me back from his first salary and cleaned up his life from that moment on.

Roan's social awkwardness lessened. He actually became a normal, well-developed person. Roan had made a choice, and followed through.

Whenever I needed a little sales page to boost conversion rates, I would design it myself and give it to Roan to add all the necessary links and publish it online. I'd pay him $100 per page, which was ridiculously high for the amount of work.

# HITTING REFRESH

As an affiliate marketer, the most exciting thing to do is refresh your screen. We call it 'hit refresh.' Especially when a campaign is working, it is exciting that every time when you hit refresh you see your revenue grow.

When a campaign is going well, every time you hit refresh, there is a few hundred dollars added to your revenue. You become like a monkey in an experiment, trained to receive food each time you press a button. Hitting refresh, is a drug of choice. When you'd hit refresh, and there is no money added, you'd freak out and get nervous.

Hit refresh, page reloads, no change in revenue, 'Oh come on, what the fuck! Dammit!'

The most nerve-wracking seconds, are when you hit refresh, but the internet connection is slow, or for some reason your browser isn't functioning properly, and it takes a little longer for the page to reload. Your heart rate goes up, your blood pressure rises, your eyes start to hurt. The thought of hitting refresh wakes me up in the middle of the night, and I can't get back to sleep until I do it. I grab my laptop, eyes squinting against the blinding light from my screen, and hit refresh just... one... time. And every five seconds after that.

The day begins.

*I believe, when I'll be on my deathbed, the last thing I'll do, is hit refresh.*

# MIND LIFT

One weekend I was in London with Jim. Kasper, my very old friend, was there with his fiancée, Sharon. I saw this on their Facebook status. I hadn't seen him since I deliberately screwed up my childhood with Alvin. I was dying to meet up with them. He was the most positive person I knew from Zwolle. I already saw on his Facebook pictures that he had lost a ton of weight and looked really fit. He wore a tank top showing developed muscles in his arm. His face looked slim, with a strong chin and cheekbones, making him look very handsome. He was full of energy and walked and talked fast. He no longer wore glasses. I guess he had gotten contacts. He looked like a different person. Fat Kasper was gone, fit Kasper came in his place.

They were excited to see me, too. We met at my regular hotel, the W at Leicester square.

I could tell they were impressed.

Kasper asked me what I was doing and how I paid for all of that, and I explained it to him. At the time he was a school teacher, but he was sick of the school system. He said the system was so slow and terrible. It drove him nuts. Also, it wasn't good for the kids. They weren't learning as fast as they should, and they weren't learning what they should. They were rehashing and repeating materials from outdated books. They were teaching kids to be average. I agreed with him. He hated it there.

Kasper told me about his journey, and it was remarkably similar to mine. He had gotten even fatter after I left. He showed me a picture of it. I hardly recognized that bloated creature. It kept getting worse until he reached the breaking point. He was sick and tired of it, and he decided to do whatever it took to change. He had experienced the extreme negative and recognized he could turn it around. Instead of accepting that he was fat, just accepting the world in the way it was presented to him and accepting the life he had, he realized he had the option to change it.

After losing weight and getting to average fitness, he never stopped. He knew he could get more, way more. The options were endless, and he was actually one of the fittest people I'd ever met at that time.

He wanted to start his own business, but the step, he felt, was too great. To quit his day job like that scared him. I told him to go for it. It might be scary. It might be uncomfortable, but do it anyway. Do it when you're scared. Good things come from doing uncomfortable things. He'd better get comfortable with being uncomfortable.

'Kasper, you can do it, man. Really, it's very possible. It's a choice you can make. You gotta make a plan, and execute. Other people are doing it, those people are not smarter than you are, so you can do it too. It's as simple as that!' Is what I told him.

'If you change your behavior, you'll change your results, Kasper. If you'll take the actions needed to create a successful business, you'll create a successful business. Don't fuck around. Figure out what works, and choose to do that. It's very simple, dude.'

'Oh man, I definitely will!' he replied.

A few months later, Kasper had written a book, How to Stick To Any Diet. A year after that, another one: Mind Lift. Kasper got in touch with me every once in awhile to ask questions on how to proceed and see if I encountered the same problems in my journey, so he could learn from them.

He posted little video clips on Facebook of himself explaining theories about effective learning and how to maintain focus that became quite popular. I saw those videos and told him right away I knew this was gonna be big. They were so good. He told me he was scared while doing them. It made him nervous to put himself out there like that, but he did it anyway. Kasper was going about this in such a creative way. His method was so different than mine, and he did it with such enthusiasm. He also became an instructor of The Wim Hof Method. This is a method developed by 'The Iceman' Wim Hof, who teaches people to withstand sub-zero temperatures by meditation, in order to advance health and focus. This gave him access to thousands of valuable people he met on these programs. We spoke about this the other day, and we agreed it was the same strategy I had with Love Systems. Gain a valuable network and leverage that network to do your own thing. He started a company called Mind Lift Learning, and it's doing very well. He gives workshops in focus and meditation. They even take ice baths and hike on snowy mountains in their underwear.

I went to one of his weekends in the mountains in Poland. After ninety minutes of breathing exercises, Kasper made me jump into a freezing cold mountain river, in mid-winter, while there was snow on the ground. At first it felt cold as hell, and I was really scared that I might honestly die from hypothermia. But after Kasper's coaching, and him telling me to keep breathing no matter what, I started feeling warm throughout my entire body. After this, I had the feeling I could take on the world, and I jumped back in. That weekend I must have jumped in that freezing cold water at least twenty-five times. I really enjoyed it. It was a truly amazing experience, and once again I saw that my own abilities were way broader than I expected them to be. When I told him how impressed I was about how he did this, how he started his company and grew his brand, he told me:

'What are you talking about, man? You were the one who inspired me to do this! After meeting you in London, you were staying in that expensive hotel and you were traveling the world, I realized it can be done. Then you helped me along the way with so much advice, I probably would not have done it without it.'

This made me feel wonderful.

'Mark, you probably don't remember this, but let me tell you another story. When I was 14 years old, I was with one kid from my class in the city center of Zwolle. The carnival was in town that day. We were looking at the rides, and neither of us had any cash so we couldn't really do anything. You walked up to me out of nowhere, handed me a hand full of money and said, 'Hey Kasper! What's up buddy! Here you go, here is 100 bucks, go have some fun man!' That was incredible to me. I felt like such a badass. You were a few years older than me so I already looked up to you. That kid I was with couldn't believe it.'

I laughed as I replied.

'Haha, holy fuck, now that you mention it, yeah I think that was one day after Alvin and I pulled off another heist and I was walking around with a few grand in my pockets. Man, that seems like ages ago, that was another life man. It's crazy you still remember that! I had already forgotten.'

'Yeah, well, that was really something, Mark.'

We both grew so much since those days. It's hard to remember that's how we were as kids. Anyway, whatever, our new lives are what counts. You're not determined by your past. You're determined by the choices you make in current days.

Kasper did show me something as well though. Not only that I can withstand freezing cold temperatures if I'd focus and keep breathing, but also that there is a different way of starting a business. When I started, I focused on making money. That was it, make money. When an affiliate network asked me what my business model looked like, I'd answer 'make money.' Once I literally typed that into an online form that they asked me to fill out.

- Question: please describe your company's business model.

- Answer: I make money.

They found this funny, but accurate. I didn't care about my reputation, I didn't care about the products I sold, I cared about revenue and profits.

Kasper on the other hand told me that he was focused on 'becoming the most trusted guy on the internet.' He wasn't thinking about making money at all in the beginning. He wanted to deliver value to others, build a reputation, then use that reputation to leverage his success. It took way longer for him to become profitable, but I can see that for him these are lasting profits. His reputation will stay forever. He showed me that you can leverage a business on reputation alone.

Kasper did something I was actually scared of doing myself, and had not done yet. He really put himself out there. 'Hey, I'm Kasper, here I am! Look at me!' is what he said to the world. Kasper is an inspiring person, and I'm happy I've been part of that. He is himself. He has always been a very trustworthy person, a warm person, a person that gave me the feeling he wasn't judgmental and he wanted to do good for people. He magnified that personality into a business.

# PRIDE

I had acquired a nice big fat bank account. I was so proud of myself, it was sickening. I was especially proud that I did it without finishing high school. When I dropped out of high school, everyone told me I was stupid and it was a stupid thing to do. The teachers and students both looked down on me, but I felt I was forced into it at the time. I had a real chip on my shoulder because of it. It was very important to me that everyone knew about my success, and knew I did it without any help from school. I was so obnoxious about it. It's embarrassing to think about the way I was behaving.

You know how Facebook shows you your old 'memories' and asks if you want to share them? Well, Facebook showed me one of my posts from back then as a memory recently. I clenched up. It was so embarrassing. It was me, laughing at everyone who finished high school and couldn't get a job, while posing for a picture in front of the pool in the garden of a villa I had rented in Cyprus.

Stefania, who was there with me, told me that I was being an idiot when she saw it. I was such a douchebag about it, but I felt like I had finally proven myself, shown everyone—all my teachers and classmates, everyone in Zwolle—that I wasn't stupid.

I'm ashamed of that behavior. At Project Rock Star I thought I had left all my old demons behind me, but they are hard to get rid of, and will show up again if you don't watch out. Luckily it didn't last long. Thank god, it was only a phase I went through. I'm never going back.

# OUT OF BOUNDS

Neverblue gave away all-expense-paid trips to their best per-forming affiliates twice a year. They called these trips 'Out of Bounds,' or OOB for short. My Groupon campaign made me by far the highest performer in international revenue worldwide. So I was extremely happy to receive my OOB ticket to Okanagan, in British Columbia, Canada. This trip was amazing.

I flew first class from Berlin to Toronto and then from Toronto in a small plane to Kelowna. It was the first time I flew first class. After this, I was ruined — only the highest luxury for me. Okanagan was beautiful. It was green and sunny. It had lakes and vineyards. Lit-erally every person I asked where I could get weed there happened to have weed in their pockets and gave it to me, for free. It was paradise. We went on a huge white luxury yacht. I spoke to Bjorn, the VP of the company. Bjorn, 40 years old, had bright red hair and freckles. He had good posture, a thin red beard around his mouth, dressed in an orange T-shirt, and smiled constantly. He was from Denmark, and I'm from the Netherlands, so we felt we had some-thing in common. The cultures are very similar.

As I stood there on that yacht sipping champagne, the sun and wind were in my face. We sailed over the beautiful clear blue water in the middle of all these millionaires, and my thoughts wandered back to Zwolle. I remembered Alvin. I remembered my teachers. I remem-bered my parole officers and judges.

I remembered my struggle, and all the work and relentless focus, and I remembered how Jim spoke to me about respect and con-vinced me not to leave Project Rock Star. I thought about Joseph, who had hypnotized me, and I thought about so many of those little choices I had made and behaviors I had learned that led up to that moment. And I thought, I made it.

After the boat ride, everyone rushed to their hotel room to hit refresh.

It was a life-changing event. I met so many great guys, and I'm still in touch with a lot of them. I'd never met so many other affiliates before, and I thought I had to connect with likeminded people and work with them to advance my business.

Günther was a twenty-three-year-old German kid. He got there by promoting dating sites on Facebook. He lived in Panama at the time, for tax purposes. He had blond hair and was a bit chubby, even though he really took care of his health. He always had a mischievous smile on his face, and spoke very fast. He spoke so fast that people found it hard to understand him.

He was very clever, and we decided to stay in touch.

# 'HELPING'

By that time, I was living everywhere. A few months in Spain, a few months in Estonia, the US, sometimes in the UK; I travelled nonstop. But most of my time was spent in Hong Kong. I considered Hong Kong my home. Stefania and I loved the Chinese food, and the vibe of the city.

Stefania was actively dropping hints that she wanted to get married. It was a tradition in her Catholic family. She'd stop at jewelry shops and say 'Wow, that is such a nice ring, right?' Or she'd show me a wedding dress: 'Wow, look at that dress, I'm just saying, it's very nice.'

I got bored with it. 'You can forget about it. I won't get married, not ever. I think marriage is fucking stupid. It's a dumb contract two people sign that has no advantages what so ever!' It was a headache I didn't need.

On the airport in New York I received a message from my mother. 'Hey Mark, I am very proud of you and everything you've achieved!' What a difference from the time when she told me she was happiest when she knew I was in jail. When I was back in Zwolle, I met up with Barry. I hadn't seen him in a while. We did some cocaine in the car. Sill, whenever back in Zwolle, I'd fall back into my stupid old ways. I told Barry about my new business and the amounts of money that I was making, and that it was actually very similar to what he was doing before, only it was online. I told him that I went on this journey of self improvement, I cut down on my drug use, and only focused on positive things in life.

'Anyone can do this,' I told him.

I thought he would be happy for me. But instead, the corners of his mouth curled down, and he stared out my car window with his eyebrows frowned. That gave me an awkward feeling. I'm not sure if it was envy, jealousy, or something else, but I didn't like the look of it.

I found it hard to deal with this, and I decided I'd make him feel better. I told him I could help him get started in this business. To me this was something anyone could do, and nothing would make me happier than helping an old friend. We were from the same background, I figured. I just had some different experiences and therefore had learned some different things. If I showed him the same things I'd seen and gave him similar experiences, he would learn the same things I had learned, and his life would change for the better as well.

On top of that, he would most likely be forever grateful to me for helping him. Only a complete asshole would not be grateful for that, and Barry was not a complete asshole. I introduced him to some affiliate networks that gave him accounts straight away. I loaned him $15k. He needed this money to get started, and he would pay me back right away as soon as he made a profit. When I looked at how much money I was making, this would be very soon.

The next week, I focused on my own campaigns. They were still going strong. I checked up on Barry. His campaigns were not profitable. In fact, he had lost $4k already. Of course I had lost some money before I became profitable as well, but not that much. However, I got the expert coaching from Ryan Buke. He did not. So I could understand why it was harder for him. It was no big deal. I figured I'd give him some pointers and tips and would see how he would do. Another week went by, and he lost another $4k. On top of that he had spent some money on 'living,' as he called it, and almost burned through my entire $15k. This was when I got worried. At this rate I would never see my money back. So I made him a deal. I would give him some profitable advertisements that he could use in smaller countries like Ireland and Sweden, as long as he stayed out of the big markets I was working in, like Germany, France and Turkey. He started to be profitable, making $500 to $1k per day.

The next time I visited Zwolle, Barry was driving a brand new BMW 5 series that he rented and showed around town. He was doing cocaine with his brother and friends, and he had some girl living with him who did not have a job. Barry lied to her about everything. His drug habit, the amount of money he had, the role he played in the business, everything. He controlled her, mentally and emotionally. It was as if she was his property. It looked as if that's really what he wanted, as if he had selected her for her personality type, the type that could be controlled. I felt bad for her. But it was not my place to say anything.

He hadn't even paid me back yet. To me, it felt like I was the one paying for his car, the cocaine, and the living expenses of this girl. Once, he drove the car to an old workplace with me in the passenger seat to show it off to his old colleagues. Two girls who worked there ran outside and were amazed.

'Oh my god Barry, is that your car?' They screamed.

'Yes, I just bought it,' he replied.

He had rented that car from my money. I was amazed and didn't even know how to respond. I had never experienced anyone being such a poser. The girls got in the car and looked around.

'Oh my god! That's such a nice car, Barry!'

Barry had a big proud smile on his face, showing his crooked front teeth. One of the girls looked at me and asked, 'Wow, such a nice car, right?' I wasn't really sure if I should play along or what. I felt uncomfortable and replied, 'Uh... yeah... it's uh... nice...' It was quite insulting seeing him show off my money to everyone and feeling so proud of it. He could at least pay me back first.

I got worried.

# FIRST WARNING

'Hi!' I see in the right corner of my MacBook's screen. I click on it, and a Skype window opens. It's Günther, the German kid from Out of Bounds.

'Hey, man, I'm in Amsterdam. Are you around?'

I wasn't. I was in Brazil at that time with Stefania.

'I moved to Amsterdam because Panama got boring to me. I just wanna stay here and smoke weed,' he said.

*Wow, cool. A fellow affiliate in my home country. Too bad I'm not in town.* I thought.

'Actually, let me introduce you to my mate, Barry. He lives in Zwolle, which is an hour drive from Amsterdam.'

I called up Barry and told him to go meet Günther. They became friends. I was in touch with Günther from time to time, and we were considering doing a project together. I tried to get in touch with Barry but he wasn't picking up his phone and was not online on Skype. He also wasn't returning my calls. After a week went by, I got really worried. *Did he disappear with my cash?* I tried to get in touch with his mother, his brother, and with friends we had in common. I even tried getting in touch with the girl that he had living with him through Facebook. Finally, his brother replied, said he spoke to him, and he would get in touch with me soon. At last, a sign of life.

A few days went by. Still no sign of Barry.

Suddenly, a week later, he messaged me 'Yo!'

It took me by surprise, I thought I would never hear from him again, and I pretty much already accepted that he stole my money.

'What the hell is going on, dude?' I asked him.

'I'm sorry man. Things just got a bit too much for me, I couldn't see straight.' I detected an apologetic shameful tone in his voice. 'I'm sorry Mark, all the cash is gone. I checked my bank account last week, and American Express took the money I owed them. I'm in the red now.'

*He blew all the cash? I gave him $15k. He almost burned through it. Then I gave him profitable campaigns that were making him up to $1k a day, and he burned through that as well?*

I should have said that, but I didn't.

'I apparently just needed this lesson, Mark. I know I screwed up. I won't make the same mistake again. I've been so stupid. Believe me, I'm in pain now, and I know it's my fault.' He said while almost crying.

I felt bad for him. Luckily, he admitted his mistake, and he told me he wouldn't do it again. Because I had made my own mistakes in the past and had learned from them, I believed him.

'My girl....' He continued in an ashamed sad voice 'She even offered to get a job to help pay the bills. She told me she doesn't mind working, and she wants to help me...'

*Oh wow, she sounds like a great person, actually. This is going in the right direction, I thought.*

'That just hurts so much.' He continued.

'Uh, what do you mean?'

'Man, it just hurts so much, my woman shouldn't be working. I am the one that makes the money. I just feel hurt as a man, do you get that? It just hurts my honor.'

*It hurts your honor? You make the money? What the hell?! That's my money, you idiot! You never made any money, and you're talking about honor? What about your honor when it comes to my money?!* I should have said this out loud, but I didn't.

This is the moment I should have said no. This is where I should have put a stop to this whole facade and been honest with myself that this guy wasn't up for it, but I didn't. I gave him $15k and a profitable business, and he spent my money on drugs, cars, and—I found out later —hookers. Barry told me he had a solution. I would help him run a new campaign, and I would keep my eye on it very closely. All profits would go directly to me until I had my money back.

'Ok man, I'll help you, because you're my friend. You're like my brother, man. I wouldn't want to do this without you. But promise me Barry, you'll quit doing cocaine entirely.'

'Yes man you're right! Our friendship means everything. Of course, we're like brothers.'

There was an excitement in his voice.

'I will quit cocaine. I'll no longer do it. Not ever!' He promised me.

'Dude, for real. If you use cocaine, even once, it's over, man. You can't build a life while on cocaine. If that's what you want to do, fine. No judgment here. But I don't want to be involved, and our business relationship will end.'

'I promise you, Mark. It's over. I've learned my lesson.' I believed him. He needed my help. He was like family.

Within a week I had $10k back. Then the campaign wasn't profitable any longer. I was sick of it, and told him to keep the remaining $5k. It was a headache I didn't need.

I remembered when I started. I had $150k in the bank, as clean profit, before I even did as much as spend $500 on a vacation. He started spending all the money he made, even before he paid back his investor, me.

Even before he had his money in the bank, he had already spent it.

This was when Stefania first told me, 'Barry is not your real friend. He only wants your money. You can't trust him, he gives me the creeps.'

I lashed out at her and got really angry.

'How dare you talk to me about my old friend like that! I've known him longer than you have! It's not your place to say anything about him!'

I should have listened to Stefania. I didn't.

# DRUG (AB)USE

Drugs became very normal, and to a lot of people they are normal. In both the poor environments as well as the rich environments I've spent my days in, there was drug use and drug abuse. All layers of society suffer from this problem.

It came down to a choice really. It was the same choice as leaving Zwolle. It starts by admitting you have a problem and deciding you need to do something about it. When I left Zwolle, my drug use became less because I deliberately refused drug abusers access to my social circle. However, it was still there. Occasionally everyone took at least some cocaine. For me, it was very hard to say no to this for a very, very long time. I wouldn't actively go out and buy it, but if someone had it on them, there was no way I could refuse. Then, if I was already on it, the craving started, and I kept wanting more and more. Not everyone had this craving I had noticed. I went too far with it before in my life. I crossed the border too many times, so my body went back into the same state as when I was actively abusing drugs.

It was exactly like an alcoholic who can never drink alcohol again, not even once. I started to fear this craving. I knew if I had one bump, that would be it. I'd go over that line. My night would be ruined if I did. I cut ties with everyone who used drugs, even if they used it only a little bit or only sometimes, and I told everyone that I would not accept drug use from anyone.

The occasional recreational joint would be OK, but even that not every day because that can be as much of an addiction as any other drug, no matter what stoners like to tell you. I still had my setbacks. Whenever I was under a lot of stress, I'd smoke weed every day, all day. At a party, if someone had cocaine, I'd sometimes still forget to say no. It was hard.

Whenever I meet a person who uses drugs, I immediately know I don't want to see this person again. This happens even among the most successful people I spend my time with now. Don't think it's only the lower levels of society. It's everywhere. I have an agreement with myself that I'll allow myself to smoke weed whenever I'm on holiday in Amsterdam; maybe a few times a year.

As with everything, if you smoke weed every day, though, it's still very harmful. Every once in awhile, after a period of heavy daily use, I'd get depressed and scared that I might have an addiction, so I'd quit. But after I'd quit I would realize that quitting wasn't that hard. *Hey, I've quit, I've done it, this was easy,* I would think. That would make me convince myself that I was probably not addicted. Because if I was addicted it should be way harder to quit. Then I would start again and tell myself there was nothing to worry about because I had 'proven' that it was not an addiction. The result would be the same, stoned and numbed every day. Whether it was an addiction or not was irrelevant.

Doing drugs is for losers. Drug users are losers. I don't want them around me. They make me sick to my stomach. If you have friends you only do drugs with, they aren't your friends. They are actually your enemies. They have a stake in you not improving your life because if you did, they wouldn't have anyone to do drugs with anymore. These people are ruining your life.

Quitting drugs is in fact very easy. There is only one thing you have to do:
- Don't use drugs.

# ARNOLD

Günther, Stefania, and I came over to Poznan. Stefania still dropped hints that she wanted to get married. It was so obvious and annoying. I told her to stop it. Günther and I had wanted to work together since Out of Bounds in Canada, and I also wanted to introduce him to the guys from Project Rock Star. We would chill in my apartment and work on some marketing campaigns. Then we would go to Project Rock Star the week after, which was held in Budapest that year, only an hour flight from Poznan.

At Project Rock Star we met Arnold, a tall, shabby-looking thirty-year old. He had curly black hair, dandruff, and a goofy looking smile with yellow teeth. He had a belly sticking out, and he slouched. He was very friendly and was in a good mood all the time. For most of his adult life, he worked in oil fields in Canada. He had been in and out of foster care when he was a kid, and recently reunited with his biological mother. He came with some baggage, but didn't we all. I really liked Arnold from the start. When he turned thirty, he decided he wanted to change his life, and did a complete 180. He quit his job and came over to Project Rock Star, without much of a plan. He knew he didn't want his old life any longer.

Günther and Arnold liked each other straight away, and Günther wanted him to come to Poznan to learn marketing from us. I found a new affiliate offer that went live in the Netherlands, KIMPORN. Users would pay a five euro-per-week subscription to view adult videos. The interesting part was the way these subscribers paid. As soon as a user wanted to view a movie on his mobile phone and tapped on 'play,' a payment window would pop up. The user would tap on 'agree' once to accept the payment terms, and a subscription would start. The user would now be billed five euro per week on their mobile phone bill. I realized I could use this type of payment for anything, Porn, Dating, Games, Gambling, and random content websites. It didn't matter. There would be only one goal — Make people tap AGREE. I didn't need this affiliate offer. This was something I could most likely do myself.

# SO SICK

I got in touch with Roan to do the technical integration of the payment screens on our websites, and decided to bring him on as a full partner. Roan, Barry, Günther, and I started the new business. Arnold was around too, but only to learn.

The company was built on my ideas, and it was mainly my money that started the business, but I gave everyone equal shares. I thought they would be more engaged if they owned equal shares, and they would be grateful to me.

Jim called me late one night.

'Mark, I have to talk to you.' He sounded serious.

'Look, man, the structure of your company, and the guys you're working with are terrible. It's extremely unstable, and it will fail.'

Jim was, and still is, the smartest person I know. He was most likely right.

'Look, this guy Barry, I get it, man. He's adorable. He is just so ridiculously dumb and has that empty-headed smile on his face all the time. It's endearing. But, Mark, you can't start a business with a guy like that. I also don't trust him. His intentions are wrong. His motivation is not the same as yours. He can't be trusted.'

He was right. However, I didn't have the stomach to pull out at that time. I'd just feel so bad. Barry was like my brother.

'Listen to your gut, man. What is your gut telling you?' I didn't see the seriousness of the situation back then. 'Who are you certain of? Who do you think you can count on 100 percent?'

'Roan,' was my answer. 'I trust Roan 100 percent. He is a hard worker, and he'd never screw anyone over. He isn't greedy. I know Roan. He is solid.'

That was what my gut told me. I should have listened to my gut, like Jim said.

When I visited Jim in London, we spoke about internet marketing. He had also met Charles, but he had not been able to get any profitable campaigns yet. He was struggling with it. I showed him an ad that I was using, and he couldn't believe it. The advertisement was almost completely unrelated to the product. I told Jim that didn't matter.

'The best thing you can do for yourself is to be very clear in what your goal is. Keep it as simple as possible,' I explained to him.

'What is your job, Jim?'

'Uh... my job is to get people engaged in the marketing campaign so they will like the product and want to buy it.'

'Wrong! Your job is to make money!'

'Holy shit, what?' Jim looked surprised.

'I don't care about anything else besides making money. I don't care if they like the products. I don't even care if they want to buy it. I care whether I get paid or not. That is my goal, so that is my job.'

Then I dropped a sentence Jim would remind me of many times after this.

'The most important part of business, is getting paid. The rest is irrelevant.'

The way I saw it, the whole attitude was actually very Zen.

'Whatever makes you money, Jim, just do that. Don't overthink it. Is there revenue? Are there profits? Yes? Go with that, then. Don't do anything else than what makes you the most money the fastest. Deal with the rest later. When the money is in your bank account, all other problems will disappear and resolve themselves. Almost every problem in life can be solved with more money. Just get fucking paid.'

Flabbergasted is how I would describe Jim's face.

He showed me an advertisement he had made.

'No man! That won't work at all!' I told him. 'Look man, you need to grab people's attention, how do you think you'll do that?'

'Uhh....'

'The headline, and the picture, that's what grabs people's attention! The ad copy can be used to persuade people to buy or sign up, but the headline and picture is what gets you the high click through ratio. The ad copy and landing page is what gets you the sales.'

'Of Course!' Jim shouted enthusiastically, 'Sick! that makes so much sense!'

He held the top of his head with both hands and smiled big, showing his teeth and gums, his eyes moving from left to right.

'Thanks man! This is sick! I can't believe it. So sick... So sick!'

'Hehe, that's cool, man.'

# WEED AND SWEAT

Roan and I were at my mom's place in Zwolle. Roan copied a random porn site onto our server and integrated the payment screen. I started a marketing campaign, and within one minute, I hit refresh, and we had our first subscriber. We were ecstatic. It felt like that time in Miami when I made my first $2. We high-fived each other, danced around the room, rolled a victory joint, and got high as a kite. I hit refresh every 2 seconds, my fingers and eyes hurt. An hour later, we had more than twenty subscribers.

Barry was moving out of his apartment to join me in Poland. He called me up one day to ask for a favor.

'Hey Mark, I've moved everything out of my place in Zwolle, but I have only a few more things I need to stash somewhere. Is it ok if I put some of my things at your mom's house?'

'How much is it?' I asked him.

'Oh, really just a few boxes, and that's it. Nothing special. Just very little.'

I agreed to this — anything to help. When I visited my mother, I learned what Barry considered to be 'only a little bit.' Two sofas, three closets, and boxes stacked up to the ceiling took up all free space in my old bedroom. There was a window in the room, buried under his clutter. I could not reach that part of the room to open or close it. All sunlight was blocked and the dust from under the sofas and between the cabinets floated around the room, making it hard to breath. The attic was blocked up with similar possessions of Barry's. Her shed was crammed so full with dismantled Ikea furniture that it became impossible to close the door. It was not a little bit. It was a lot.

Everyone except Roan, who still worked at ASML, moved to Poznan to work on this company. We were sure we would all be millionaires within one year. Günther and I were the only investors in the company. But soon Günther ran out of money, or so he told me, and I was left as the only investor and kept adding money to the company. My money went fast. Arnold gave a whole lot of valuable ideas, and we considered making him a partner as well.

Stefania hated that period. Everyone was always over at each others houses, smoking weed. A few times a week our entire apartment smelled like weed and sweat. Stefania was angry that she had to live in that situation. That would then make me angry at her, for being angry at me. Barry wanted Stefania to be friends with the girl he was seeing, but Stefania didn't like the way Barry was treating her, and thought that she was an idiot for accepting it.

The whole company was financially carried by my savings, and I lost sleep over it. I was always tired and smoked weed all day with Barry. It's what we connected over, smoking weed. Because of all that, my relationship with Stefania suffered.

'You're an idiot, Mark! Those guys are using you! You are letting them take advantage of you, and also me!' She screamed one day while we had a huge fight. Tears smeared her black mascara down her cheeks all the way past her chin.

'Fuck you! How dare you say those things?!'

My face turned red. I was resisting the urge to smash things.

'Everyone is working hard here! We all want the same and everyone has to make sacrifices!'

'You're stupid, Mark. Those guys are only out to use drugs and fuck hookers, FROM YOUR MONEY!! You are not like that. You are more serious, you are a better person than they are!' She cried and stormed out the apartment.

'A better person?! What kind of stupid thing is that to say?' I shouted after her while she ran down the stairs of our apartment building. I slammed the front door shut.

Stefania and I broke up. She moved in with her cousin, and we were not in touch any longer. This felt strange and empty, I tried to numb it with weed, but it only made it worse.

Günther was sick of Poznan. So we all decided to go to Marbella, Spain. The guys would go over there first. Roan and I would arrive later. I told Barry he had a certain budget to get us a car. A BMW 3 series would be fine and would fit the slim budget we had.

He called me.

'Hey, Mark! I would not be Barry if I had not gotten us the BMW 5 series for the price of the BMW 3 series,' he said, sounding all proud of himself, trying to make it seem as if his negotiation skills had gotten us a massive discount. Soon I found out that was not true, he just wanted to drive a bigger car. He lied about the price to me. I started to get annoyed with his bullshit.

Roan called. 'Mark, Barry called me. He wants me to create a website, but I'm working on the payment system. He got angry, but he just doesn't seem to understand that if the payment system doesn't work, it doesn't matter how many websites you get up. People won't be able to pay. Is this guy an idiot or something?'

I knew he was an idiot. *He didn't fucking know that a tree was a plant.* It's just that I felt Barry and I had a lot in common; not just the fucked up relationships we had with our fathers, but also our drug use. We had such a history together, and I had made such progress, I felt I owed it to him to help.

A few days went by and Arnold called me one evening. 'Mark, I'm in Marbella.' He sounded tired. 'Barry and Günther just went out, I think they are fucking some hookers.'

'Hey man! Haha really? How's the weather there? In Poland it's fucking rainy, I can't wait to come over there dude.'

'Yeah, the weather is nice, it's sunny all day. But, Mark, it's Barry. He has become very bossy. Since you're not around he has become impossible to deal with. I can't work like that.'

'Arnold, come on, man. I know, I keep hearing the same from people, but you know, Barry, he is just one of those guys we keep around for the atmosphere. I love that guy. He just cracks me up.'

'Mark, I don't know how much of this I can take.'

I understood what Arnold was trying to tell me, but Barry was like family to me. He was my best friend. I knew him since my days in Zwolle, and I wanted to grow in life with someone I knew from my childhood. It made me feel great to share a brotherhood with someone that came from the same place as me.

'Arnold, believe me, sometimes I'm just sick of his bullshit too. The other day he lied to me about the costs of the car. It actually pissed me off a lot. But I don't think he means anything by it. I think he is just a bit stupid sometimes, but it's funny though, he doesn't really think things through.'

'I fucking hate that guy. He is a dominant asshole.'

'Look man, he is making changes and he is just adjusting. He promised me he'll change. He is even quitting cocaine. Come on, he deserves a chance.' I told Arnold, doing my best to stick up for Barry when people seemed to be turning on him.

Arnold replied, 'Quitting cocaine? What the hell are you talking about? This guy is on cocaine every day. He is literally the biggest coke-head I've ever known. He just doesn't do it around you, and he hides it really well.'

My mind went blank. I needed time to process this. Suddenly everything started to add up, all the pieces of the puzzle fell into place. Slowly it dawned on me, Barry was playing me, and everyone else. I went silent for a minute, but it felt like seconds to me. I couldn't find the words to describe my thoughts and feelings.

'Hello? Mark? Mark, are you still there?' Arnold thought the connection had died.

I snapped out of it. 'Dude... Are you fucking serious?'

'Yeah man! Günther thinks Barry has it all figured out, but I seem to be the only one that sees he is a lying coke-head loser! I've seen him buy drugs using company money with my own eyes!'

'Dude...'

'To you, especially, he just pretends to be someone else all the time. He is not who you think he is, Mark. He doesn't act like himself around you. He knows you have the ideas and the cash, you are his ticket, so he is very careful around you...'

'Wow, dude. Wow.'

My world shattered. Barry had been lying to me, about everything. He was not my friend, he was a parasite that figured out a way to drain money from me, and I let him. He lied to his mother, to his brother, to Günther, his girlfriend, everyone. I knew this. I've seen it. So why would I think he didn't lie to me?

I shook with anger.

*Fucking Barry.*

# ALONE

I stayed alone in my apartment in Poznan. It gave me lots of time to think about my life, and how I felt about it all. For two months I had been without Stefania. It felt lonely. Thoughts about her were going around in my head. I was so angry at her, but the anger faded over time. It turned out she was right about everything, and I felt like a real idiot. When I calmed down, I missed her feminine energy. I knew she was a sweet and caring person, and I wondered if I hadn't made a huge mistake. Now that we had plans of going to Spain, I started to worry I might never see her again.

Luckily, she felt the same way as I did. She missed me as well, but wasn't ready to just get back together like that, and needed to know I really understood what I did wrong. We talked about it for weeks, and decided to make some choices. She wanted me to be more serious in our relationship, as well as in my business. She was looking out for me. She could see what type of people I associated with, and it wasn't good for me. I was starting to understand that she might have been right all along.

In those stressful days, I realized she was the best thing in my life. *Who the fuck was I, that she wanted to be in a relationship with me?* She moved back in, and, finally, I was happy again.

# FUCK THOSE GUYS

Roan quit his job, and we drove to Marbella the following week. Stefania and I first drove from Poznan to Nijmegen to pick him up, and then we drove from there to Marbella, stopping to sleep at motels along the way. We spoke nonstop about the whole situation. It drove Stefania crazy.

Roan and I decided to leave the company. It was a very tough decision, but we knew it was the right one. We wanted to give Günther and Arnold the chance to go with us, but they didn't. Arnold wanted to, but didn't have the nerve to leave Günther.

'You were trying to screw out Barry!' Günther screamed with his face turned red.

*My god, he has no clue*, I thought. Barry had the same emotional hold over Günther as he had over me, I could see it. He had already picked his next victim.

The corners of Barry's mouth curled down, his eyebrows frowned; 'You fucking cripple,' he mumbled.

Usually when people are angry at me, but I haven't done anything wrong, they try to attack me on what they think hurts me most, my arm. What they don't understand is that to me, that is proof I did nothing wrong. If I did something wrong, he would have attacked me on that. They deserved sixty percent of the company money, they said, because there were three of them and two of us. Günther and Barry owned equal shares in the company. I gave them those shares as a present, and now they felt they had the right to demand shares of the company money. My money. I fucked myself.

Back in the hotel, I created an excel sheet, and I added the value of everything I owned at that point in my life — my apartment, and cash in different currencies. Excel calculated the sum of it all for me, and there at the bottom was my net worth. It didn't look good. I had made so much money before, but my investments in this company and Barry almost made me broke. Me trying to help almost drained all wealth from me. All that money, gone!

I was lied to, and it left me in a bad spot, financially, and worse, emotionally.

# IDIOT TAX

Jim called. He was in Gibraltar, an hour drive from Marbella.

'Hey Mark, do you have a printer?'

'Yeah man, I have a printer.'

'Wow really? Does it work?'

'Uh, yeah dude, of course.'

'Oh my god, sick! Sick! Can I use it?'

'Haha yeah of course, man. Well, it's not sick, it's just a printer...'

'Oh my god! Sick on so many levels!'

We drove there and I told him what had happened.

'Didn't I tell you that was going to happen? What did I say, Mark? What did I fucking tell you?' he replied.

He was right. It was exactly what he said would happen. Jim was constantly on the phone, talking to accountants and his team members. He desperately needed a printer to print and sign contracts for his thriving business. Turns out, he had become very profitable online after what I told him about affiliate marketing. He told me that after the conversation we had about it, a huge light bulb went on in his head and he absolutely crushed the market.

He reminded me of my own words. 'The most important part of business is getting paid.' He had hired two interns to run his marketing campaigns for him, and he travelled the world making deals with businesses to sell their products online. Jim, just like Kasper, showed me that there is another way to run a business than what I've been doing. Kasper showed me that a business can be built on a good reputation alone. Make sure people know and like you, and leverage that into profits.

Jim showed me that the way I was running the business can be leveraged by hiring the right people and multiplying your revenue tenfold. When I started, my goal was to make a couple of hundred grand and then chill out and smoke weed. When Jim started his goal was to build a huge business and make multiple millions. I was thinking too small. He said he'd be forever grateful to me for what I'd done for him and his whole team.

I kept telling them that if it wasn't for Jim, I would not have done anything. If it wasn't for that talk he gave me in Stockholm about respect, I would not even have been able to speak to Ryan Buke, and I would not have been a Love Systems instructor. Heck, if he hadn't started Project Rock Star, I would never have met Charles Ngo. I was happy I could return the favor.

Jim told me that most likely Günther and Barry justified what had happened in their own way. That had dawned on me before as well. They must have their side of the story. He told me it was in my best interest to make a deal with them about the money as soon as possible, and be gentle, because this could get ugly. I went over to their house. Arnold opened the door. He looked like he was in agony, wearing a white T-shirt covered in brown stains. He had wet spots under his armpits. One foot wore a white sock that had turned grey and black around his toes and heel. The other foot was naked on the cold floor with hairy knuckles and long yellow toenails. He told me he was depressed.

The shades were down and it smelled like that drug dealer's house where I met Amy. There was left over weed and cocaine on several spots on the coffee table and dresser. Barry and Günther were out to score some more drugs, he told me. We had a long talk, and I could see that Arnold was a very clever, very reasonable person, who had made the wrong decision and was with the wrong people. This looked very familiar to me, so I couldn't blame him. I made a deal with Arnold to split the cash fifty-fifty. Roan and I would get half, and the three of them would get half, plain and simple. We were giving Arnold and Günther their share, and Barry nothing. That's how we saw it. If Arnold and Günther then decided to give Barry some of their money, that was up to them. We gave them an extra 2.5 percent. They got 52.5 percent because we figured they were paying 'idiot tax,' as we called it. Any money going to Barry was taxation for partnering with an idiot. I know I paid my fair share of that. After being very angry, we broke all contact and did not speak to them again.

An aggressive voice in my head told me to take revenge. I felt betrayed and taken advantage of. After sending a bunch of angry emails, I understood that doing nothing was the best course of action. The best revenge is to live well.

That was all my own fault. No need blaming Barry, or anyone, for this. He is who he is. He can't help it. Just like those thugs back in Zwolle that robbed me. They were assholes, but I could have prevented it. I always thought Barry was not really an asshole. He was just a bit stupid and it wasn't really his fault. Then I thought that no one was that stupid, and he must be doing it on purpose, so actually he was a huge asshole. Roan pointed out that it was most logically a combination of the two: a stupid asshole.

I had created this. I made the choices leading up to this, even if it was with the best intentions. Barry had already showed me countless times that he was not the sharpest tool in the shed. Showing the world how much money he had was more important to him than actually having the money. Every time I made a wrong decision in trusting a person or company, there always was this voice telling me that I was making a mistake. I think the most valuable thing a person can do is learn to listen to this voice. I've learned to listen to my gut now. I don't need a rational explanation. Whatever my gut is telling me, I know it to be the right move. Barry was a leftover from an old life — a negative aspect I was not ready to let go of yet. In a way, he stroked my ego and reminded me of where I came from. He never made the choice to change. I was the one that wanted him to change, he didn't want to change at all. Wanting to help him and continuing to push him forward was a way for me to feel good about myself, not because it was necessarily the right thing to do for him. He made me feel better about myself.

Barry: a drug of choice.

# GETTING PAID

We focused 100 percent on work again. Roan and I made an agreement that I would make the marketing as aggressive as possible to have the highest profits we could get. We launched our websites in several more countries like Germany, Brazil, and South Africa. I hit refresh more than there were minutes in a day.

A new affiliate network arose in the Netherlands, Advidi. When I started, they didn't even exist. In the short period they have been in the game, they have grown up to become one of the biggest networks out there. I was intrigued.

One of Jim's guys introduced us and they gave me an account. I looked for similar offers that we had been promoting ourselves. With our knowledge and experience, it was a piece of cake for us to set up these campaigns for other companies as well. They didn't have many back then, especially compared to now, but I created the best advertisement campaign I could think of for the one offer I could find and launched it on Facebook.

The next day I got a Skype message from my affiliate manager Hardy: "Mark, have you seen your earnings per click? They are amazing. How are you doing this?"

I looked at my revenue. It was over $2k. My average earnings per click was $3, which is high compared to the average - $0.20.

"Hey Hardy, I don't share my campaigns, my man ;)" I didn't know these guys. Why would I share this info with them? Their job is to get us paid; how we are getting the sales is none of their business. It wouldn't be the first time an affiliate network stole a campaign from their top affiliate. I'm not falling for that one. After I got to know them better, I realized he was only trying to help out... but I wasn't taking any chances.

Hardy replied, "Ok, that's fair enough. What do you need from me? How can I help you scale this?"

"Well, Hardy, you guys don't have many offers that are optimized for mobile phones. Can you get some more? It would really help me if I could get a few more of these offers to maximize results."

Hardy replied quickly and clearly: "I'm on it!"

When I opened my email inbox the next day, it was crammed full of emails from Advidi. They had been very busy reaching out to hundreds of companies all over the globe to get me mobile offers to promote... UK, Netherlands, Germany, Portugal, Italy, Belgium, Scandinavia, South Africa, Thailand, India... the list went on. Roan and I went to work. We sat behind our laptops for weeks. I hit re-fresh more times than there are minutes in a day. We traded sleep for money.

Hardy did the same. It didn't matter if it was 3 a.m. on a Sunday morning; he was always available to help us squeeze as much out of our campaigns as we could. He was the best affiliate manager I'd ever worked with. He told us it was because of Advidi's work ethic. "Help affiliates make as much money as humanly possible, do what-ever it takes, and make sure everyone gets paid - no matter what!"

The most important part of business is getting paid. They under-stood this. We understood each other. It's no wonder these guys are so fast, I realized.

Hardy emphasized it once again. "Understand this, Mark: we make sure our affiliates get paid, no matter what! We don't care what we have to do or who we have to fight. We will make sure they get their money. That is our job. That's what we do. You just create the marketing campaigns and get the sales any way you can. We will do the rest!"

I learned more, once again, from seeing this team of people work so hard, with such a great company culture. It inspired us to do the same. It motivated us to reach for the stars. Advidi was a big part of our success, and it was more than financial. They really cared about how I felt while working with them.

Roan and I both moved to Hong Kong. Within three months, our monthly revenue exceeded $400k, while our costs were almost non-existent. It was almost all profit. We were rich.

Roan moved to Bangkok after this and stayed there to live like a king. I went with Stefania to San Diego to hang out with Ryan Buke and his partner, Mike, for the time our tourist visas would allow it. San Diego was great. People were saying it was America's finest city. I haven't seen all of America, but of what I've seen, I must agree.

We rented a Mustang convertible with New York license plates. Once a guy pulled up next to us and shouted 'You guys should go back to New York!' We laughed.

'We'll be sure to do that, buddy!' I responded. He drove off.

A new Project Rock Star started in Las Vegas, which was only an hour or so flight from San Diego. Everyone was there. Jim was there with his whole team. He introduced me to a guy named D, who he told me had campaigns that did $250k per day on Google AdWords, selling diet pills. Normal is what you decide it is.

Jim got us one of the most expensive suits in the Cosmo, for a fraction of the price, using his contacts. We went to a party in XS nightclub, He paid $30k, just for the table near the DJ. Jim asked me if we could split the bill 3 ways.

Stefania heard this and told me, 'If you'll pay $10k to get into a club, I'm going home. Are you crazy? I don't care how much money you have, Mark, you're not doing that!'

Back at the hotel I created an excel sheet. It was 8 months since the last time I had done this. I added the value of everything I owned at that point in my life — my apartment, my stocks, bonds, commodities, gold, silver, and cash in different currencies. Excel calculated the sum of it all for me, and there at the bottom was my net worth — it was almost two million dollars.

We crushed seven countries with our own mobile offers, combined with the excellent collaboration with Advidi, we made more money than we even considered possible before.

I was excited and anxious at the same time. I couldn't sit still. It felt amazing.

The following morning, I snuck out early to get Stefania a present. I woke her up.

'Baby, wake up, I have a surprise.'

'Huh, whaaaat?' She whispered slowly while opening her eyes. She looked at the big pink box with black ribbons around it that I placed next to her on the bed. 'Oh baby, what's this?'

She opened the box and took out the Agent Provocateur lingerie set inside. Her eyes dilated. 'Oooohhhh that's so nice, thank you baby.' She smiled and looked at the present from both sides. A price tag fell out.

She grabbed the tag.

'$1660?!' She screamed.

'Oh shit, that was not supposed to be in there.'

'Are you stupid, Mark? Where is this shop?'

'Well, I just wanted to be nice.'

'There is being nice, and there is being dumb. I will go there and see what I can do.'

She showered, did her make up, dressed up, took the present with her, and went to Agent Provocateur. When she returned, she told me that she exchanged it for store credit, and showed me a pink card. A week later she bought the same set back when it was on sale, including two other sets that were all massively discounted. After this she still had store credit left to buy a few more.

She was right, that was way smarter.

# GETTING SUED

Stefania and I arrived at Schiphol airport in Amsterdam and went to my mother's house in Zwolle for some well-deserved sleep. I parked my pearl colored BMW below the hill in front of the house. We wanted to stay there for a few days before going back to Hong Kong. We were going to bed, I opened my laptop and checked my email. There was an email from the telecom regulator in Germany. When I opened it, my heart started pounding.

It was an official order to change our service and to deliver proof of consent by our subscribers. There were screenshots of the payment screens we'd used, saying the price wasn't clearly visible on them, and it wasn't clear enough to consumers that it was for a subscription. He wanted to know how many times we had used this payment screen. I was wide awake at that point. We had travelled more than twenty hours. Stefania was dying to go to bed, but I was not getting to sleep any time soon. I called up the regulator. I told him I did not have all the information, and I'd have to have my technical guys look at it.

Adrenaline shot through my body. I got sweaty. I was scared we'd have to refund everyone and pay a huge fine on top of that. We'd be bankrupt.

*I'm just back where I started*, I thought. I was in Zwolle, at the same house I was living back in my early days. The same house I was in with Alvin after our first successful heist. The same house I lived in all those times the police came looking for me. *I'm in trouble again. I haven't changed a bit.*

While lying on my bed, I actually cried. I was so scared. Stefania was comforting me. It helped a bit. It was a completely new situation for me — the type of situation I always feared, where I'd have to defend myself against a regulatory organization, an organization that could ruin me if they wanted to. I had made the agreement with myself long ago that I would do things that scare me, even if I'd have to do them while scared. Now, when shit finally hit the fan, I was really scared.

I called Roan and told him about the email. He was as nervous as I was. This was unknown territory, and it scared the shit out of us both. We made up a list of subscribers that, as far as we knew, were signed up using that payment screen. We sent this to the regulator. According to him, the best we could do is send all of them an sms informing them they could get a refund if they wanted. We decided to stop promoting our services after this to avoid any more trouble. We already had such a huge database of subscribers that our income would still be very high.

This went well for a couple of months until we received another email from the same regulator. This time, he ordered us to shut down the service. He ordered the company that processed our transactions to no longer pay us and hand over all the screenshots of every payment screen we had ever used in any transaction.

Apparently one of the mobile operators had found another faulty subscription that was not on the list I gave him. I called our payment processor and spoke to the CFO. He laughed a bit. He was CC'd on the same email, so he knew the story from the start. Looking at our payment screens, he agreed with the regulator that they were against the code of conduct.

The regulator told him I had lied to him before, and he was pissed. He took it quite personally. I turned white. I rambled my entire side of the story to him.

'Ok, calm down...' he chuckled.

There was a commission hearing in Munich, Germany. I put on a suit and went there. The regulator was there, and he was actually a nice guy. I really liked him. Two weeks later we received the verdict from the commission. A record fine, for these types of services, in Germany. I won't disclose the amount, but it was way less than I thought it would be. They also told us to not give any refunds. Weird.

All this time I had been worried sick, but this fine was a joke. Our payment processor was still holding quite a lot of our money, more money than the fine, so we even got wired some extra cash after this. We seriously laughed and went out for champagne that night. The decision not to give refunds was a strange one. Effectively, you could translate the verdict into this:

'We find it proven that consumers have been paying too much for your services, and that you deliberately tricked them into this. But don't give them back any money, just give some of that money to us, and we'll call it even.'

No one else really thought this was a big deal. Just business as usual. It's all part of the game. I should have known this earlier. It would have saved me a lot of headache. So, once again, the same attitude paid off.

*When you're afraid, do it while afraid, but do it.*

# THAT'S FRESH, BRO

Stefania and I started traveling again. Stefania had given up on marrying me, and was fine with it. She realized it wasn't something I was willing to do, and accepted it. I liked that. She stopped dropping hints, and never mentioned it in any conversation. When a family member asked her about it, she replied 'no, we aren't getting married, that's stupid. Our relationship is strong enough, we don't need a marriage.' It gave me the feeling she was really with me, for me. Not because she wanted to get married, but because she wanted to be together. Any stupid tradition or contract was irrelevant.

We went to Zwolle for a few months. It was such a long time since I'd been there. Now Zwolle seemed like a darling little town to me. The old churches and canals, it had a charm I couldn't fully appreciate when I lived there as a kid. In Zwolle, we usually drove around in a pearl colored BMW convertible in the summer and a black Jaguar in the winter. People I knew from back in the day couldn't believe their eyes. There was such a difference in life style. I didn't even expect it would be such a big deal. To me this was all normal. But the biggest difference I noticed was in conversations with people — the problems they had and how difficult they found it to solve them. These issues were peanuts to me. I had created and overcome so many problems, but these people were still stuck with the exact same problems they had when I left. These people never went out into the world to challenge their own beliefs, question their habits, or build character.

One snowy day, we went to get a vegetarian burger in the center of Zwolle. I parked the Jaguar around the corner from the burger place. After picking up our food and walking back to the car, I heard a familiar voice behind me shouting, 'Hey, Mark!' I looked back, and it was Bernie's son, Michael. He looked dirty, like he hadn't showered in weeks. His skin was dry and damaged. He looked like he was drunk and on other drugs. He was drooling and found it hard to focus his eyes. He was homeless.

'Hey, man, how are you doing?' I asked him. Stefania pulled my arm.

'Come on. Let's go. What kind of person is this? Please let's go.'

She was scared. To her, this was a creepy homeless junky, who she would never get in touch with. She didn't even comprehend how I knew this guy.

He tried to mumble some words to me, but I could not understand him. He blew bubbles with his spit while he tried to talk. I saw Stefania was really creeped out, so I decided to open the car door and get inside. We drove away.

I used to see this guy every day. I smoked weed with him and used other kinds of drugs. He was homeless, mumbling to himself. I drove away in a brand new jaguar. *How the choices we make in life make a difference. My god.*

I was relaxing at a coffee shop the following summer. I sipped my cappuccino, wearing my sunglasses, enjoying the weather. I looked up, and saw Barry. He was surprised to see me. He was dressed in a blue blazer that was too small for him, the buttons looked like they were about to snap, and his sleeves were too short. His trousers were stained and crumpled, as if he wore them from the day before.

'Heyyyy Barry! How are you doing?' I asked him with a big smile on my face. The corners of his mouth curled down again, and his eyebrows frowned.

'I'm doing very well! Very well!' he shouted while looking grumpy and angry, making me wonder how accurate that was. Usually people who are doing well don't get angry when you ask them how they're doing. I told Roan. We had a good laugh about it.

Ryan came over to Europe after the sale of his company. We spent some time in Warsaw together. It was the first time Ryan left the United States; he was such a typical American.

'Wow bro, there are so many people in the world, bro. It's amazing. Look at that girl at the bus stop, just looking at her phone, not giving a fuck about the U.S. at all. That's crazy, bro!'

In Amsterdam, Stefania, Ryan and I rented an Airbnb in the city center. Stefania and I had been together for six years by that time. She stuck by me in horrible times, and in great times. When I was almost broke, or very rich, she was there. She stuck by me through addiction, a time in my life of which I wonder how anyone could stand to be around me, but she did. She told me truths I didn't want to hear when I needed it. Whenever I wanted to waste large amounts of money, she told me I was an idiot and she wouldn't accept it. Most of all, she was with me for me. She had proven to me that she was the person in my life that would be there for me, no matter what.

I snuck out one early morning to go to Koster Diamonds, and bought her an engagement ring. Exactly the type of ring she showed me when she thought I wasn't paying attention. When I came back, she was still in bed and asked me where I went so early.

'Oh, I just went to get a lighter and smoked my joint.'

She looked at me angry from under the thick white blanket, 'Why did you smoke weed so early in the morning? Are you stupid?' She rolled over and went back to sleep.

She had no clue. That evening, I told Ryan he was on his own, and I took her to one of the top Michelin star restaurants in the city, with a beautiful view over the night life of Amsterdam. This is where I asked her to marry me. She couldn't believe it.

She said yes.

I asked Ryan to be my best man.

'Of course, bro! That's fresh, bro!'

# GROWING

When you decide to grow, leaving some people behind is inevitable. These people won't like it. They will feel left behind, and some of them will take it as though you think you are better than they are. Of course you don't think that. It's just that you feel you are better than the person you were at that time, and that you deserve more for yourself.

They can decide the same thing and put in the same work if they want to, but they have to really want it. It's up to everyone to evolve, or not. It's their choice, and their responsibility.

When your friends are all junkies, they don't want you to stop using drugs. If you do, they will feel left behind and alone in their bad habits.

This is an extreme example, one that I personally experienced, but it is even applicable to something as simple as deciding not to play video games all weekend, but to study instead, or work on your company.

Those are not your real friends. That's something you'll have to come to terms with, and do it fast! A lot of friends I've tried to help hate me now. I know it's because I put too much pressure on them to become something they weren't ready to be. Then I found it hard to deal with it myself when they didn't live up to my expectations and fell back into old habits.

The cases where I loaned them money are the worst examples of that. I found this very hard to deal with. But let my advice to you be to accept this as soon as you can. Recognize who wants the best for you, and who wants you to grow. Recognize who wants you not to grow, and wishes you'd stay in the safe little comfort zone with them where there is little room for improvement.

You'll be out of touch with them because it will become harder to even have a conversation. As you learn, your interests will broaden and your understanding of yourself will outgrow theirs. The contact won't be the same. It hurts, but that's the way it goes. It's their decision. We all start out at different points in life, so we all have our own paths of learning. I had to learn so much through trial and error. Every time something went wrong, I felt horrible and stupid. But in the end, those are learning moments, and I should be happy that I've had the opportunities to experience them.

The only way not to make mistakes is by doing nothing and being nothing.

Every time I made a choice to grow in my life, the people around me didn't understand it, and called me stupid.

When I was selling drugs, I decided to not take revenge after being robbed, and people around me called me a pussy and an idiot. When I moved to Poland, everyone said it was the dumbest thing to do. When I went to Love Systems, people said I was 'getting suckered into something.' When I decided to dedicate myself to internet marketing, and quitting comics, they said the same thing. I won't even go into the retarded shit people said when I decided to stop eating meat.

People are scared of change, and can't handle growth. It's a mindset trap, don't fall for it!

I realized something. By being back in Zwolle, in the same environment I was in when I was a criminal and drug addict, a life that now was so far from my current one, something hit me. Something that made me feel great.

*Regular people, don't have this life.*

*Regular, normal, everyday people, who have jobs and live normal lives, don't make money online, travel the world, sleep in expensive hotels. Regular people don't buy apartments and pay for them in cash. Regular people don't spend an average annual salary on an engagement ring. Regular people don't have this kind of freedom.*

*This is something that I created, with my choices and behavior. Just like I chose to be put in prison, and robbed by drug dealers. In the same way I choose the life I have now.*

*Make no mistake. I created this.*

# EPILOGUE

Roan and I are still working together on different projects. We're back in Hong Kong. I have an actual office where I hit refresh all day.

We have some employees now, and we are moving forward. Our marketing team promotes affiliate offers and generates sales online. We create apps, games, quizzes, everything that makes us money. Our company did a million dollars revenue in one month recently. We keep discovering that there really is no limit to the amounts of money you can make. I have made so many great friends, and I'm thankful for the life I've had so far.

The best affiliate network I currently work with is Advidi, from Amsterdam. I love their mindset of success and creativity. They protect their affiliates and are an absolute pleasure to work with. My affiliate manager, Hardy, is considered a close friend of mine, and is invited to my wedding. I love those guys.

I'm excited about what the future will bring. If I compare where I came from, and how I started, to where I am now, I'm amazed by the progress a person can make if you just go for it. Set aside your anger and fear, focus on developing your good sides, and let go of toxic people in your life.

The first time I told Stefania about the way I used to be, when I grew up in Zwolle, she laughed. She could not believe it.

'You, in prison? Haha! Of course! Hahaha you hurting people? Haha! No way! You are too cute for that, don't make me laugh!'

This is a very good thing. It shows me how far I've come. People from my current life cannot believe the way my life used to look. It's so far from who I am now, they can't imagine it in a million years. Old friends from Zwolle cannot believe the way my life looks now. They consider it almost impossible. It's very far out of their reality.

Bas, Kasper, Frank, and I are friends again. With Bas I even have a tradition to share a hotel room in Amsterdam on valentine's day. Don't ask why.

I'm myself now. Now I'm the person I was supposed to be all along. Not that I'm done growing, no not by far. It still is a constant evolution and struggle. It's two steps forward, one step back, then two steps forward again, hopefully.

Someone from my old life told me recently that he 'hopes I don't forget where I came from.' Well, to be honest with you, I kinda want to forget. Those days sucked and didn't do me any good. Those people sucked as well. The only good thing that came from it was that I screwed up so badly I recognized I had to run in the opposite direction, far away from that place.

It made me come to understand that if you choose to behave a certain way, you'll get certain results. If you choose to behave in the opposite way, you'll get opposite results. Just know that it's always your choice, and it's always your own behavior that is either the problem or the solution.

I want to continue building a social circle of positive people — people I can learn from.

Like Jim told me recently:

'Who do you win around, Mark? What people help you grow? Spend your time with those people!'

*I will.*

Mark & Stefania 2017

Made in the USA
San Bernardino, CA
15 March 2017